STEP·BY·STEP
cake decorating

STEP·BY·STEP
cake decorating

KAREN SULLIVAN

Penguin
Random
House

Project Editor Martha Burley
Project Art Editor Kathryn Wilding
Managing Editor Dawn Henderson
Managing Art Editor Christine Keilty
Senior Jacket Creative Nicola Powling
Jacket Design Assistant Rosie Levine
Producer, Pre-Production Sarah Isle
Producers David Appleyard, Jen Scothern
Art Director Peter Luff
Publisher Peggy Vance

Cake Decorators Asma Hassan,
Sandra Monger, Amelia Nutting

DK INDIA
Senior Editor Charis Bhagianathan
Senior Art Editors Ira Sharma, Balwant Singh
Editor Janashree Singha
Assistant Art Editors Tanya Mehrotra, Aastha Tiwari
Managing Editor Alicia Ingty
Managing Art Editor Navidita Thapa
Production Manager Pankaj Sharma
Pre-Production Manager Sunil Sharma
Senior DTP Designer Jagtar Singh
DTP Designers Satish Chandra Gaur,
Rajdeep Singh, Rajesh Singh, Sachin Singh,
Anurag Trivedi, Manish Upreti

This edition published in Great Britain in 2013
by Dorling Kindersley Limited
80 Strand, London, WC2R 0RL

Copyright © 2013 Dorling Kindersley Limited
A Penguin Random House Company
6 8 1 0 9 7
025 – 193751 – Oct/2013

A CIP catalogue record for this book
is available from the British Library.
ISBN: 978-1-4093-3481-1

Colour reproduction by Altaimage LTD
Printed and bound in China

A WORLD OF IDEAS:
SEE ALL THERE IS TO KNOW

www.dk.com

Contents

Introduction

CAKE DECORATING has enjoyed a huge surge in interest over the last few years, with enthusiastic beginners creating celebration cakes, exquisite cupcakes, and perfect cake pops in their own homes. This trend is possible thanks to the multitude of tools and specialist ingredients that are now available, and the help of decorating classes, blogs, websites, online videos, books, and programmes that are devoted to the subject. We are no longer afraid to bake, and our creations are becoming more sophisticated and adventurous as time goes on. But how do we get started? What do we need to know to create beautifully decorated cakes with that perfect finish?

This is the ideal book for anyone who wants to learn how to make spectacular cakes of their own. With its unique user-friendly structure, detailed step-by-step instructions, and exciting projects, it guides and inspires as you master the basics.

An introductory illustrated **Tools and equipment** section shows you what you need to streamline and enhance the process of decorating cakes. Get prepared with a chapter devoted to techniques for preparing and using your **Key ingredients**, such as flower paste, marzipan, fondant, buttercream icing, tempered chocolate, and royal icing to pipe or ice. Continue with over 100 clear step-by-step **Decorating techniques** – all of which include tips from the experts to make them both failsafe and achievable. With over 20 simply glorious **Projects** from three award-winning cake designers, you'll find everything you need to make special celebration cakes with great success. Finally, in an expansive **Cake basics** chapter, there are delicious recipes for cakes in a wide variety of flavours, textures, shapes, and sizes, and instructions for making them work – every time.

Like all skills, cake decorating can take some time to learn and a little patience to master. Some techniques are simple, others require practice. All, however, will help you to create original cakes, cupcakes, 3D creations, and cake pops that are sure to thrill your family and friends.

Happy decorating!

Decoration choosers
Floral

Ruffled cake
pp224–25

Filigree wedding cake
pp214–16

Blossom stencil cake
pp205–07

Cupcake bouquet
pp198–99

Cigarillo wedding cake
pp210–12

Wedding mini cakes
p213

Heart-shaped posy cake
pp200–01

Gerbera

Cymbidium orchid

Orchids, cornflowers,
and baby's breath

Purple roses

Creating flowers and sprays
pp90–91

Butterflies and blossoms
pp184–85

Children's

Princess cake pops
p175

Teddy bear mini cakes
pp190–91

Princess castle
pp170–75

Dinosaur cake
pp167–69

Train cake
pp164–66

Pirate cake pops
p179

Scary cake pops
p189

Halloween pumpkin cake
pp186–88

Rabbit

Cow

Baby ladybird

Pirate ship cake
pp176–79

Teddy

Modelling characters
pp94–95

Novelty

Handbag cake
pp202–04

Sports' ball cakes
pp180–82

Suitcase cake
pp208–09

Gingerbread house
pp194–95

Ballerina

Football
player

Modelling characters
pp94–95

Elegant

Shades of pink
pp196–97

Blossom stencil cake
pp205–07

Calla spray

Creating flowers and sprays
pp90–91

Damask

Stencil designs
pp132–33

Cigarillo wedding cake
pp210–12

Ruffled cake
pp224–25

Occasions

Filigree wedding cake
pp214–16

Christmas cake pops
p223

Newborn celebration cake
pp192–93

Halloween pumpkin cake
pp186–88

Festive yule log
pp218–19

Poinsettia

Creating flowers and sprays
pp90–91

Tumbling teddies

Stencil designs
pp132–33

Valentine's hearts

Festive stars

Plunger cutter designs
pp104–05

Cigarillo wedding cake
pp210–12

Festive fruitcake
pp220–22

Tools and equipment

Almost all of the different effects, textures, decorative touches and, indeed, perfect finishes for professional cakes rely on the use of specialist tools and equipment, now widely available. Assembling a toolkit of these essentials can make cake decorating so much easier.

Baking and assembling

Prepare a flawless cake with the help of specialist tools for baking, icing, stacking, and presenting.

Dowels *are cut to size and used to support heavy decorations or multiple cake tiers.*

Icing scrapers, *with different edges, help to achieve a smooth or textured finish with buttercream or royal icing.*

Cake-pop sticks *come in a variety of lengths and are used to support decorations.*

Non-stick fondant mats *help to measure, roll, and cut fondant, dough, or other modelling pastes.*

Fondant rollers *are essential for ensuring that fondant, flower paste, and other modelling clays are smooth and evenly rolled.*

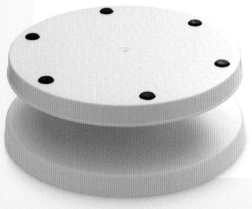

Turntables *not only make icing cakes easier, but allow you to access all sides with a quick spin.*

Separator plates *snap together and help to create balanced, supported tiered cakes.*

Sugar thermometers *check the temperature of ingredients such as tempered chocolate and spun sugar.*

Pillars *separate and provide support for cake tiers. They come in many different styles.*

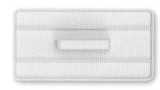

Fondant smoothers *smooth decorations, boards, or cake toppings. Use two to achieve crisp corners and edges.*

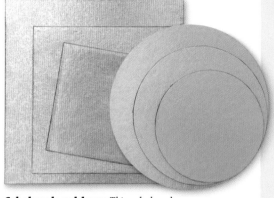

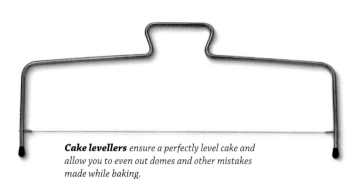

Cake levellers *ensure a perfectly level cake and allow you to even out domes and other mistakes made while baking.*

Cake boards and drums *Thin cake boards support individual cakes for multiple tiers. Thicker drums provide a sturdy base.*

Moulding and embossing

Use one of a number of different moulds to produce two- and three-dimensional decorations, and decorate the surface of cakes and decorations with the use of embossers.

Resin moulds *ensure that detailed decorations, such as lace or facial features made from fondant or modelling pastes, hold their shape.*

Crimpers *add design features, decorative shapes, and texture to fondant.*

Veiners *help emboss veins and provide shape to fondant or flower paste leaves.*

Embossing mats *are used for rolling fondant. Press the paste into the surface for a variety of textures.*

Silicone moulds *are used for chocolate, flower paste, and fondant.*

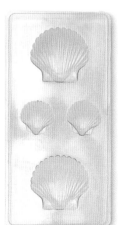

Plastic moulds *are ideal for large creations, especially those made from tempered chocolate.*

Embossing rollers *are used to emboss the surface of decorations or fondant cake coverings.*

Cutting

It is easy to cut detailed or simple shapes accurately with the help of specialist cutters. Many play a dual role, as they can emboss while cutting your medium to shape.

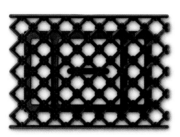

Plunger cutters *create crisp shapes that are released with the touch of a button. Some also emboss the surface.*

Patchwork cutters *help emboss the surface of cakes and decorations, or cut out detailed designs that can be painted, dusted, or layered.*

Multi-ribbon cutters *make cutting accurate lengths and strips of fondant or other pastes easy. Choose the width and fix the frame with interchangeable cutters that can emboss and/or cut decorative edges.*

Tappit cutters *are perfect for small, detailed decorations. They can cut out fine shapes like letters and numbers and emboss a design on the surface.*

Cutting wheels *help cut fondant, flower paste, and other pastes quickly, easily, and accurately. Many come with multiple heads for different effects.*

Metal cutters *help cut accurate shapes that can be layered or used as the basis for decorations. Many come in sets of multiple sizes.*

Modelling

Adding detail and modelling decorations is easy with the help of many tools that can create different effects. You can purchase the essential tools (see opposite) in a set.

Flower formers *allow you to dry fondant or flower-paste flowers and other decorations in a concave shape, and support your creations as you apply detail to the surface.*

Flower picks *are hygienic tools to help you insert fresh or wired floral decorations into the surface of a cake.*

Flower nails *provide control while piping. Rotate one between your thumb and forefinger to turn it as you pipe flowers onto the surface.*

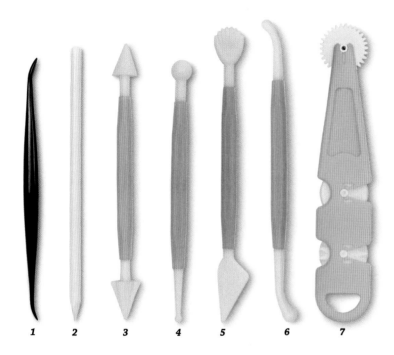

1 Veining tools, also known as Dresden tools, add detail to fondant or paste decorations.

2 Frilling tools can be rolled across thinly rolled fondant to create frills and ruffles.

3 Cone tools create detail and texture. They double up as star embossers.

4 Ball tools can thin and soften edges to create natural petal shapes and contours.

5 Shell and blade tools emboss shell patterns and texture, and can cut or shape.

6 Bone tools smooth curves when modelling, and cup and frill flower petals.

7 Stitching (quilting) tools emboss decorations and cakes with stitching effects.

1   2   3   4   5   6   7

Florist's wire comes in a variety of different "gauges". Use it to produce sprays of decorations, such as hearts or stars, and to wire flowers and foliage.

Florist's tape is used to cover the surface of florist's wire. Tape together wires to create stunning displays of flowers and leaves.

Flower mats help to shape petals and foliage with soft curves and additional detail, such as veining, and provide an excellent surface for drying.

Piping

Piping can be used for a wide range of decorative work, including icing cupcakes, lettering, trimming, and embroidering. Build up a collection of tips (also known as nozzles) to make decorating easier.

Round tips *are versatile and widely used. They come in many sizes, from tiny tips for piping dots, embroidery, and lettering, to wider tips for prominent effects.*

Petal tips *are available in many sizes, and help to create realistic flower petals, as well as ruffles, drapes, swags, and bows with royal or buttercream icing.*

Couplers *allow you to change tips without emptying the piping bag.*

Closed star tips *help to pipe ruffles on cupcakes or mini cakes, as well as buttercream swirls and shells.*

Open star tips *are perfect for piped borders, single drops of stars and flowers, and swirled cupcakes.*

Piping bags *come in a variety of sizes. Choose larger ones to pipe buttercream icing on cakes or cupcakes, and smaller ones for more detailed work with royal icing.*

Leaf tips *have v-shaped openings, perfect for pointed ends on leaves. You can pipe them flat, ruffled, or as 3D creations.*

Drop flower tips *help to create flowers with one squeeze of the piping bag. Different cuts determine the number of petals.*

Shell and rope tips *are used to create ropes and shell borders in varying sizes, scrolls, and other borders.*

Multi-opening tips *are ideal for stranded details or beads, and scallops.*

Basketweave tips *are serrated on one side to produce ribbed, wide stripes of icing.*

Ruffle tips *have a teardrop-like opening that produces a range of ribbons, swags, and ruffles.*

Piping bottles *with small tips help to pipe chocolate and thinner royal icing, or to drizzle designs on the surface of cakes, cookies, and cake pops.*

Painting

Use pens, edible dusts, inks, and even glitter to add colour, create detail, and add an exquisite finish to your cakes and decorations. Paint freehand, or with the help of stencils or an airbrushing machine.

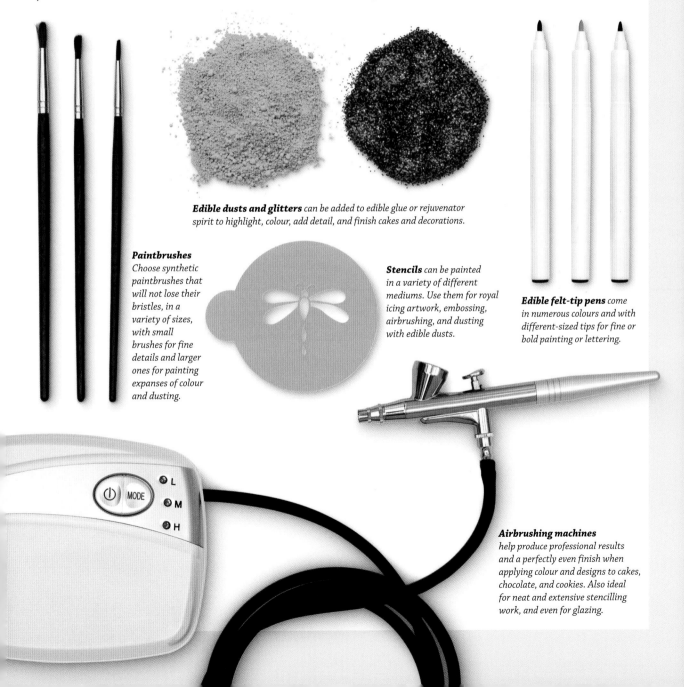

Edible dusts and glitters *can be added to edible glue or rejuvenator spirit to highlight, colour, add detail, and finish cakes and decorations.*

Paintbrushes
Choose synthetic paintbrushes that will not lose their bristles, in a variety of sizes, with small brushes for fine details and larger ones for painting expanses of colour and dusting.

Stencils *can be painted in a variety of different mediums. Use them for royal icing artwork, embossing, airbrushing, and dusting with edible dusts.*

Edible felt-tip pens *come in numerous colours and with different-sized tips for fine or bold painting or lettering.*

Airbrushing machines
help produce professional results and a perfectly even finish when applying colour and designs to cakes, chocolate, and cookies. Also ideal for neat and extensive stencilling work, and even for glazing.

KEY INGREDIENTS

*A few basic ingredients form the building blocks of cake decorating.
Find out how to prepare these ingredients, flavour or colour them
to your preference, and use them to ice, cover, and texture a cake.*

Buttercream icing

This type of icing is made with butter, icing sugar, and cream or milk, and is lightly flavoured with vanilla or another flavouring. Use it to ice and fill sponge cakes and cupcakes. Some buttercreams require cooking, but most can be whipped up quickly with an electric whisk.

Basic vanilla buttercream icing

You can make this with or without cream or milk. It is ideal for crumb coating, icing sponge cakes, and for piping onto cupcakes. You could also use it for brushwork embroidery (see p139).

 **PREP** 15-20 mins

 **MAKES** 750g (1lb 10oz)

Ingredients

* 250g (9oz) unsalted butter, softened
* 2 tsp vanilla extract
* 600g (1lb 5oz) icing sugar
* 2 tbsp double cream or milk, plus extra for thinning
* colouring paste, optional

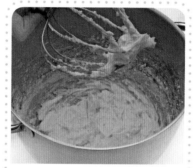

1 Cream the butter and vanilla together with an electric whisk. Add the icing sugar, beating well.

2 Beat in the cream and continue mixing until the icing is light and fluffy.

3 Transfer to a bowl and add colouring paste, a little at a time, until you get the right colour.

4 The icing should be firm enough to hold a knife upright, but soft enough to be piped.

Rich, creamy, and fluffy, *buttercream icing is ideal for icing and decorating sponge cakes.*

Ingredients

For chocolate buttercream
* basic ingredients (see opposite) plus:
* 8 tbsp cocoa powder

For lemon or orange buttercream
* basic ingredients (see opposite) plus:
* finely grated zest and juice of 1 lemon or 1 orange

For coffee buttercream
* basic ingredients (see opposite) plus:
* 2 tbsp strong coffee, such as espresso, cooled

For cream cheese buttercream
* basic ingredients (see opposite) plus:
* 200g (7oz) full-fat cream cheese, drained in a sieve

Chocolate buttercream

This icing works well with dark chocolate cakes. Follow steps 1–2 of the basic vanilla buttercream recipe. Add the cocoa powder and beat until fluffy. Use milk instead of cream in step 2 and beat until smooth. If you prefer a lighter flavour, halve the amount of cocoa powder, and add it at step 1, before you whisk.

Lemon or orange buttercream

This zesty buttercream is perfect on a vanilla sponge. Follow step 1 of the basic vanilla buttercream recipe, omitting the vanilla. Instead of adding cream, use lemon or orange juice in step 2, beating until smooth. Add the lemon or orange zest, mixing continuously.

Coffee buttercream

This icing has a light coffee flavour that can be deepened by using stronger coffee. Follow step 1 of the basic vanilla buttercream recipe. Use only 1 tablespoon of cream and add the coffee, beating until evenly distributed, light, and fluffy. For a slightly marbled appearence, lightly whisk in 2 tbsp coffee powder instead.

Cream cheese buttercream

This icing will be looser and creamier than a basic buttercream, but sets nicely. Follow step 1 of the basic vanilla buttercream recipe. Omit the cream and add the cream cheese, a little at a time, beating vigorously until fluffy. Keep 300g (10oz) extra icing sugar to hand and add more to achieve the consistency desired.

Italian meringue buttercream

Rich, smooth, soft, and creamy, meringue buttercreams can be flavoured with extracts or a dash of citrus oil. Egg-based buttercreams like this are trickier to make and are too soft for detailed piping. The end result is well worth the effort, though, as they are great for piping cupcakes.

 **PREP** 25 mins

 **COOK** 15 mins

 **MAKES** 900g (2lb)

Equipment

* sugar thermometer

Ingredients

* 5 free-range pasteurized egg whites
* 300g (10oz) caster sugar
* 500g (1lb 2oz) unsalted butter, softened
* flavouring, optional

1 Place the egg whites in the bowl of an electric mixer and beat until foamy with soft peaks. Whisk in 50g (1¾oz) of the sugar, a little at a time, and mix until firm peaks appear.

2 In a medium pan, add the remaining caster sugar and 90ml (3fl oz) water, and heat over a low heat. Swirl the pan gently to help the sugar melt and then turn up the heat to medium. Bring to the boil and cook until the sugar thermometer reaches 121°C (250°F). Remove from the heat.

3 Continue to whisk the egg mixture using the lowest setting and pour in the sugar syrup, running it down the side of the bowl. When the bowl is cool to the touch, add the butter, 1 teaspoon at a time. Keep whisking. If the mix is runny, keep on adding butter until smooth and stiff. Stir in flavouring, if using.

Variations

Try other buttercream icings: German buttercream involves making a pastry cream by heating eggs, milk, sugar, and cornflour, straining, and then beating in butter. French buttercream is a richer variation, and uses egg yolks rather than whites.

Italian meringue buttercream *should be smooth and stiff. Add flavours when the texture is right.*

Rolled buttercream

Rolled buttercream is a softer, shinier type of malleable icing. It has similarities in texture to traditional fondant, but it is so much tastier. It can be flavoured with cocoa powder, if desired, used to cover cakes and cookies, and strengthened for decorations (see p87).

 **PREP** 20 mins

 **MAKES** 1.5kg (3lb 3oz)

Equipment
* dough hook, optional

Ingredients
* 250g (9oz) unsalted butter, softened
* 240ml (8fl oz) golden syrup
* ½ tsp salt
* 1 tsp vanilla extract
* 1kg (2¼lb) icing sugar, plus extra for dusting

Tip
Rolled buttercream does not keep for quite as long as traditional fondant, and will need to be stored in the fridge in an airtight container. Before rolling, warm it gently with your hands and knead on a surface dusted with icing sugar.

1 In a large bowl, whisk together the butter and golden syrup until smooth and well-blended. Mix in the salt and vanilla extract. Gradually mix in the icing sugar, a little at a time, until the icing becomes stiff.

2 If you have a dough hook, attach it now and use it to knead the icing until pliable and smooth. If the icing is sticky, add a little more icing sugar.

3 If you do not have a dough hook, turn out the icing onto a board dusted with icing sugar and knead it by hand.

4 To use, roll the icing out to the required thickness on a clean surface, dusted with icing sugar, and apply to cakes or use for decorations in exactly the same ways as fondant (see pp46–51).

A dough hook *can help with the effort of kneading rolled buttercream.*

Filling a layer cake

Cake layers always need levelling before you fill them (see p239). Sandwiching thin layers makes a sponge cake sturdier and easier to carve. Ganache (see p38) can also be used to fill cakes, as can whipped cream, jam, and fruit curds. Avoid overfilling, and allow the filling to set before icing.

Equipment
* cake board
* turntable or lazy Susan
* piping bag with large, round tip

Ingredients
* cooled cake layers, levelled
* buttercream icing (see pp24–25)

Cake layers always need to be levelled before filling

LAYERING CAKES
Carving and covering cakes **p65**
Building tiered cakes **p68**
Building with pillars **p69**

1 Place the base layer and board on a turntable, levelled side up. Fill the piping bag with icing and pipe around the inside edge.

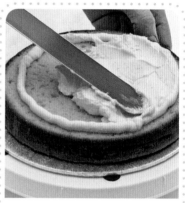

2 Using a spoon, place a large dollop of icing in the centre and spread to the edges with a palette knife, until smooth.

3 Place the next layer on top, levelled side down. For 2-layered cakes, you are now ready to crumb coat and ice. To build the cake higher, repeat, with the next layer levelled side up and then the levelled side down. You could finish with a levelled side down layer, for a level surface.

Crumb coating a cake

Crumb coating is like adding a base coat to a wall before painting. It helps to ensure a perfect finish for iced or fondant-covered cakes. It smoothes over any cracks or holes in the surface and helps the cake stay sealed and moist. You can crumb coat with buttercream or, if desired, ganache (see p38).

Equipment

* cake board
* turntable or lazy Susan

Ingredients

* cakes, levelled, and layers filled with buttercream icing
* buttercream icing (see pp24–25), thinned with some milk

...ensure a perfect finish for iced cakes

CRUMB COATING CAKES

Carving and covering cakes **p65**
Building tiered cakes **p68**
Building with pillars **p69**
Building asymmetrical cakes **pp70–71**

1 Place the cake on a board, on a turntable. Use a palette knife to carefully apply a thin layer of buttercream to the cake.

2 Start at the top of the cake, and swirl the buttercream over the surface as you turn it around on the turntable.

3 Spread the icing around the sides until evenly covered. A few crumbs may be embedded in the icing; this is normal.

4 Refrigerate or allow to dry – this can take up to 2 hours. Apply the final layer of icing (see pp30–31) or fondant (see p50).

Icing a cake

This method works best of all with buttercream icing, although you could use ganache (see p38) or whipped cream. Use tools, such as serrated scrapers, to create a variety of textures as you ice. A textured look can be achieved by spreading the icing in swirls, rather than smoothing with a hot knife.

Equipment

* cake board
* turntable or lazy Susan
* untextured kitchen paper
* scraper, flat-edged

Ingredients

* buttercream icing (see pp24–25)
* cake, levelled, layered, and crumb-coated (see p29)

...achieve a textured look by spreading the icing in swirls

ICING CAKES

1 Dot a small amount of buttercream on the cake board and centre the cake on top. Place on a turntable and dollop a large amount of buttercream icing into the centre of the cake.

2 With a palette knife, swirl and smooth the icing, spreading it outwards and over the sides as you go.

3 Turn the cake as you spread the icing down and around the sides of the cake, to cover it as evenly as possible. When it is smooth, allow the cake to set for about 10 minutes, and then repeat.

4 Fill a glass jug with boiling water and insert a palette knife blade into it. When it is hot, dry it and run it around the sides, turning the cake around with the flat surface of the knife against the icing. Repeat till smooth.

5 Make the top smooth with a hot knife, turning the cake with the flat surface of the knife against the icing. Move from one side of the cake to the other. Allow the cake to set for about 15 minutes.

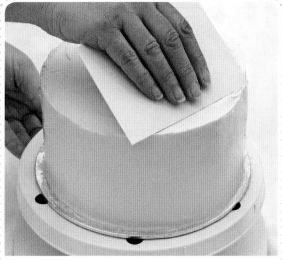

6 Place a sheet of untextured kitchen paper on the surface and "polish" the cake so that the surface is smooth. Use a scraper to smooth the icing all the way around the cake, if desired.

Piping cupcakes

You could ice a cupcake with buttercream icing using a palette knife, rotating it on a flat surface as you spread. For a quick, professional-looking finish, however, pipe the buttercream into a swirl, as shown here. You could use different tips for stars, shells, or a variety of effects and textures.

Equipment
* piping bag with large open-star tip

Ingredients
* buttercream icing (see pp24–25)
* cooled cupcakes
* sprinkles or edible glitter, optional

...use different tips for a variety of effects and textures

PIPING WITH BUTTERCREAM
Making a piping bag **p73**
Filling a piping bag **p74**
Piping buttercream borders **p78**
Piping a buttercream rose **p79**
Piping lettering **p84**

1 Attach the tip to the piping bag and fill it half full with medium-consistency icing. More makes the bag difficult to handle.

2 Hold the tip 1cm (½in) above the cupcake, at a 90° angle, and pipe from the outside edge inwards, in a spiral.

3 Apply pressure so that an even quantity is released. Slowly increase the pressure at the centre, so that the icing forms a peak.

4 Release the pressure to end the spiral at the centre of the cupcake. Decorate with sprinkles or edible glitter, if desired.

Filling cupcakes

Cupcakes can be filled with jam, buttercream icing, ganache, cream, or even loosened peanut butter, fruit mousses, and curds. Pop in a marshmallow or another treat before filling, for an extra surprise. There are two successful methods for filling cakes with liquid ingredients.

Cone method

With a sharp paring knife, cut out a cone shape from the centre of each cupcake. Slice off the tip of the cone, fill the cone-shaped cavity in the cupcake to just below the top, and then replace the flat end of the cone on top. Proceed to ice as usual (see opposite).

Piping method

If you have thin, smooth icing or jam, you can use a plain round tip (pictured below) or a specialized injector tip on a piping bag. Attach the tip, load the piping bag with filling, and then insert it into the centre of the cupcake, from the top. Gently press on the bag until the filling begins to expand out of the insertion hole. Proceed to ice and decorate as usual (see opposite).

Using a piping bag helps to control the amount of filling you use.

Tip
Always make sure the cupcakes are completely cool before attempting to fill them or they will fall apart. Cooling will also ensure that the filling will not melt into the cupcake, making it soggy and messy to eat.

Royal icing

Make this sweet icing with egg whites, icing sugar, and lemon juice. It is traditionally used to ice fruitcakes for weddings or Christmas, and to decorate gingerbread houses. With a few changes to the recipe, it can be used for decorative piping (see pp73–75) and "runouts" (see pp140–41).

Traditional royal icing

Royal icing dries hard, so keep it covered with cling film or a damp towel while you are working. The glycerine in this recipe stops the icing from becoming rock hard, and provides a little shine.

 **PREP** 15 mins

 **MAKES** 750g (1lb 10oz)

Equipment

* scraper or serrated scraper, optional

Ingredients

* 3 free-range pasteurized egg whites; albumen powder, mixed with water; or meringue powder
* 700g (1¾lb) icing sugar, sifted, plus extra if needed
* 1 tsp lemon juice
* 2 tsp glycerine
* fruitcake, levelled and layered if desired, covered with marzipan

1 Whisk the egg whites in a large bowl until they are foamy. Add the icing sugar a spoonful at a time.

2 Stir in the lemon juice and glycerine, and beat until stiff, thick, and peaks begin to form.

To ice a cake, add more icing sugar to thicken, if necessary. Use a palette knife to spread on the top and sides of your cake, as you would with buttercream icing (see pp30–31). Use an icing scraper, as shown with a mini cake, to provide a smooth finish. Try a serrated scraper for a uniform texture.

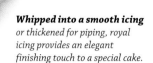

Whipped into a smooth icing
or thickened for piping, royal icing provides an elegant finishing touch to a special cake.

Tip
Fill the piping bag with royal icing (see p74), and keep the remainder covered. The icing will last up to 2 weeks, so long as it is well covered and refrigerated, but you may need to mix and thicken it with icing sugar before using.

Royal icing for piping

This recipe is very similar to traditional royal icing, but it does not contain glycerine. This makes it more appropriate for detailed piping work and gingerbread houses, when it needs to dry hard.

 **PREP** 20 mins

 **MAKES** 700g (1½lb)

Ingredients

* 3 free-range pasteurized egg whites
* 1 tsp lemon juice, plus extra if needed
* 700g (1¾lb) icing sugar, sifted
* colouring paste, optional

PIPING WITH ROYAL ICING
Building with gingerbread **pp66–67**
Basic royal icing piping **p75**
Piping dots, beads, and flowers **p80**

1 Whisk the egg whites in a large bowl. Stir in the lemon juice. Gradually add the icing sugar.

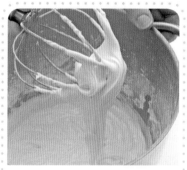

2 Continue to beat until the icing has a smooth, toothpaste-like consistency.

3 Add more lemon juice if it is too thick. Dip a cocktail stick into the colouring paste, if using. Add just a dot of colouring paste at a time, as a little goes a long way. Mix into the royal icing and stir until you achieve a uniform colour.

Marzipan

Marzipan is a thick, sweet almond paste that is traditionally used to cover fruitcakes underneath royal icing or fondant. It is also a great medium for modelling and even moulding decorations for cakes. Its high sugar content allows it to last for months without refrigeration.

 **PREP** 20 mins    **MAKES** 900g (2lb)

Ingredients

* 175g (6oz) golden caster sugar
* 300g (10oz) icing sugar, sifted, plus extra for rolling and kneading
* 450g (1lb) ground almonds
* 1 tsp vanilla extract
* ½ tsp orange juice
* 2 eggs, beaten

1 Mix both the sugars and ground almonds in a bowl. Make a well in the centre and add the vanilla extract, orange juice, and eggs.

2 Use a palette knife to gently fold the wet ingredients into the dry ingredients, until you have a crumbly dough.

3 Dust a flat surface with icing sugar and knead the marzipan until smooth, adding more icing sugar, if necessary, to achieve the right consistency.

Tips

Marzipan can be coloured in the same way as fondant (see p47). Knead a dab of colouring paste into the marzipan. Marzipan has a soft texture and will dry hard without a strengthener. Keep decorations in an airtight container once dry.

Almond-rich marzipan *provides a succulent layer of sweetness on fruitcakes. You can model it into a variety of shapes.*

Tip

Apricot glaze seals cakes and provides a sheen. It is made by mixing 200g (7oz) of apricot jam or preserve with 3 tablespoons of water. Gently heat in a small pan until warm and stir in 1 tablespoon of brandy. Sieve, and brush onto cakes.

Covering a cake with marzipan

Traditionally, fruitcakes are brushed with brandy and apricot glaze to encourage the marzipan to adhere to the surface. Marzipan-covered cakes should rest for between one and seven days before being iced.

Equipment
* cake board

Ingredients
* 20cm (8in) fruitcake
* apricot glaze
* icing sugar, for dusting

...apricot glaze encourages marzipan to adhere

COVERING WITH MARZIPAN

Carving and covering cakes **p65**

Building tiered cakes **p68**

Building with pillars **p69**

Building asymmetrical cakes **pp70–71**

1 Place the cake on a cake board. Use a pastry brush to cover it with apricot glaze (see Tip).

2 Roll out the marzipan into a circle 40cm (16in) in diameter, and 1cm (½in) thick.

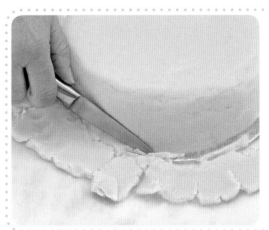

3 Lift it over the top of the cake so that it is centred, and smooth it over the top, pushing out any air bubbles. Press the paste down around the sides. If it cracks, pinch it together or patch it with excess. Rub it with your fingers to smooth. Trim off excess.

Chocolate

A versatile ingredient that you can use for many decorating techniques, chocolate can be temperamental. Whether you make ganache to ice cakes, melt and temper to create delicious decorations, or prepare a batch of modelling clay (see pp44–45), follow instructions carefully.

Making ganache

Ganache is simply chocolate melted into cream, which is then whisked to silky perfection. It can be poured over a cake while warm, or left to cool and spread with a palette knife (see opposite).

 **PREP** 5 mins

 **COOK** 5 mins

 **MAKES** 500g (1lb 2oz)

Ingredients

* 200ml (7fl oz) double cream
* 200g (7oz) good-quality dark, milk, or white chocolate

Variations

For a sweeter flavour, try milk chocolate, but allow a longer time to set. You can chill ganache and make into truffles, whip into a fluffy icing, or whisk into buttercream for an even richer icing. Make white chocolate ganache in exactly the same way.

1 Break the chocolate into pieces and place it with the cream in a medium heavy-bottomed pan. Stir over a low heat until the chocolate has melted.

2 Remove from the heat, transfer to a heatproof bowl, and whisk until glossy and thick. Pour over the cake or leave to cool for 1–2 hours before spreading.

Melted chocolate *is the basis of a host of icings, moulded decorations, and other embellishments.*

Tips

For a smooth ganache surface, dip a knife into hot water, dry with kitchen paper, and then run over the surface of the cake. You could use a knife or scraper to create textures. Try marbling with dark or white chocolate ganache.

Covering with ganache

Ganache is a popular alternative for those who find buttercream too sweet. It can be poured over chilled buttercream for a smooth layer, or spread onto a cake that has been levelled and filled.

 **TIMING** 20 mins

Equipment

* cake drum or board
* turntable or lazy Susan

Ingredients

* 2-layer cake, cooled and levelled (see p29)
* 1 quantity ganache (see opposite)

COVERING WITH GANACHE

Carving and covering cakes **p65**

Building tiered cakes **p68**

Building with pillars **p69**

Displaying sugar flowers **p160**

Displaying fresh flowers **p161**

1 Place the base layer of the cake on the cake drum, over a turntable. Spread a good quantity of soft ganache over the top with a palette knife. Place the next cake layer on top.

2 Drop a dollop of ganache over it, spreading it around. Apply a little more to the centre and repeat, bringing it down the sides. Turn the cake as you hold the flat side of the palette knife against the ganache. Continue to spread until smooth (see p31).

Melting and tempering chocolate

Whether you want to wrap a cake (see Variation, opposite), use moulds to create decorations (see pp120–23), or make curls or cigarillos, you must melt and temper chocolate so that it becomes hard and glossy. The recipe below makes enough to wrap a cake or to fill three large moulds.

 **PREP** 5 mins, plus cooling

 **COOK** 10 mins

 **MAKES** 500g (1lb 2oz)

Equipment
* sugar thermometer

Ingredients
* 500g (1lb 2oz) good-quality milk, dark, or white chocolate

...provide a hard, glossy finish

USING MELTED CHOCOLATE
Using chocolate moulds **p60**
Cutting chocolate shapes **p61**
Piping with chocolate **p85**

1 To melt the chocolate over a pan, break it into squares and place in a dry, heatproof bowl. Bring a pan of water to a simmer.

2 Set the bowl over the pan. The base should not touch the water. Make sure there is no space between the bowl and the pan rim.

3 Stir occasionally to distribute the heat. Heat until the sugar thermometer measures 45°C (113°F).

4 Remove from the heat and allow to cool until the temperature reaches 27°C (80°F), stirring frequently.

Melting and tempering in a microwave

This takes less time than the traditional method but it may take some practice, as you will have far less control of the heat. As with the traditional method, it is best to use a specialized sugar thermometer to test the temperature regularly. Overheating will cause the chocolate to take a "white bloom" once hard.

 **PREP** 5 mins, plus cooling

 **COOK** 5 mins

 **MAKES** 500g (1lb 2oz)

Equipment
* sugar thermometer

Ingredients
* 500g (1lb 2oz) good-quality milk, dark, or white chocolate

Variation
To wrap an iced cake, spread tempered chocolate over acetate that is a little larger in size than the circumference of your cake, and a little wider than its height. As the chocolate begins to harden, wrap it around the cake. When it is hard, remove the acetate.

1 Break the chocolate into squares, place it in a microwavable bowl, and heat on full power for 30 seconds. Stir, and heat again in 15-second bursts until the chocolate is smooth and melted.

2 Test the temperature and continue to heat in short bursts until it reaches 45°C (113°F). Allow to cool until the temperature reaches 27°C (80°F), stirring frequently. The chocolate should remain at this temperature as you use it, for instance for wrapping a cake (see Variation). Warm it a little if it drops too low.

Making chocolate curls

You can make curls with chocolate that has just been melted, but more attractive results are achieved with tempered chocolate (see pp40–41). Apply more or less pressure with your knife or scraper, to vary the thickness. Scraping right through to the paper gives a full, steady curl.

 **PREP** 10 mins, plus cooling

 **COOK** 10 mins

 **MAKES** 12–24 curls

Equipment

* scraper or metal spatula, optional

Ingredients

* 200g (7oz) good-quality dark, white, or milk chocolate, melted and tempered (see pp40–41)

Tips

For chocolate shavings, use a vegetable peeler to "peel" shavings from a square of chocolate, in short, firm strokes. Use a cheese shaver for bigger shavings or curls. White and milk chocolate are softer and much easier to use than dark chocolate.

1 Spread the chocolate over baking parchment on a baking tray. Tap the tray to release air bubbles. Chill until just hard.

For small curls, use a knife to scrape the chocolate towards you, forming curls with the blade. If it is too hard, let it warm a little first.

For large curls, use a scraper to push the chocolate away from you, digging right through the surface.

2 Lift the curls with a skewer to avoid leaving fingermarks or melting the chocolate, and refrigerate until required.

Painting chocolate leaves

Create realistic foliage for moulded or modelled chocolate flowers, or add a simple embellishment to cakes by painting melted chocolate over fresh leaves straight from the garden. Choose fresh, non-poisonous leaves, and wash and dry them before using.

 **PREP** 15 mins, plus cooling

 **COOK** 10 mins

 **MAKES** 12 large or 24 small leaves

Ingredients

* 200g (7oz) good-quality dark, white, or milk chocolate
* 12 large or 24 small, non-poisonous leaves
* royal icing or edible glue, optional

Variation

For cigarillos, paint tempered chocolate over an acetate square. Leave 5mm (¼in) unpainted at an edge. Roll it, press the 2 painted edges together, and tape the unpainted edge to the outside. Cool. Freeze for 15 minutes, and slit the tape to reveal a cigarillo.

1 Melt and temper the chocolate (see pp40–41). Dip a pastry brush in the chocolate and paint it over the back of a leaf. Place it on a plate or a sheet of baking parchment to cool and harden. Repeat with the other leaves. Apply more layers of chocolate for thicker leaves.

2 When the chocolate has hardened, simply peel off the real leaf by bending back the stem. The chocolate leaf will be revealed. You could apply to cakes with a little melted chocolate, a dab of royal icing, or some edible glue.

Chocolate modelling clay

This malleable medium allows you to create sculptures, ribbons, swags, and figures with ease. Unlike tempered chocolate decorations, it dries firm and has no risk of melting. It is too firm to cover a cake with, but if you want to wrap a cake in chocolate, you could use flavoured fondant (see p46).

 **PREP** 15 mins, plus hardening    **COOK** 10 mins    **MAKES** 450g (1lb)

Ingredients

* 400g (14oz) dark, white, or milk chocolate
* 200g (7oz) golden syrup

Create decorative chocolate touches with ease

MODELLING WITH CHOCOLATE

Modelling a rose **p88**
Modelling a tulip **p89**
Modelling a basic figure **p92**
Modelling embellishments **p96**
Using multi-ribbon cutters **p118**
Using silicone moulds **p120**

1 Melt the chocolate in a large heatproof bowl over a pan of simmering water. In a small pan (or the microwave) heat the golden syrup until runny and warm. Pour into the melted chocolate. Remove from the heat.

2 Stir together until the chocolate and syrup form a ball and come away from the sides of the bowl. You may need to add more syrup, depending on the cocoa content of the chocolate. If it takes a long time to form into a ball, add a little more syrup.

3 Tip the ball onto some cling film, and wrap carefully. Leave to harden for 2–3 hours. Avoid getting water anywhere near the clay, as it will cause it to mark and separate – giving your decorations an imperfect finish.

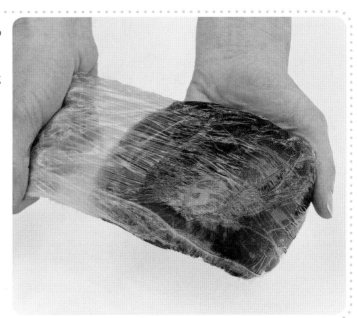

Tip

Chocolate clay will keep in the fridge for several weeks, but keep it wrapped to avoid contact with moisture. Don't worry if it cracks a little while chilling – once kneaded at room temperature, it will regain the appropriate consistency.

4 When it is hard, break some off and knead it with your hands until it is pliable. Use it to fill silicone moulds (see p120) or to model figures, flowers, swags, and other shapes. If the chocolate hardens, simply knead it again and the warmth of your hands will easily soften it.

Chocolate clay *is a great medium for modelling ribbons and bows (p96).*

Fondant

Fondant, also known as sugarpaste, is a versatile product. Use it to cover cakes and drums, and to create stunning decorations. It can be coloured, flavoured, cut, embossed, and used in moulds. If you do not want to make it, buy in any colour from cake-decorating suppliers.

Traditional fondant

This is a classic recipe that works well for all types of fondant creations. It will keep for weeks if wrapped tightly and stored in an airtight container.

 **PREP** 20 mins

 **MAKES** 1kg (2¼lb)

Ingredients

* 2 sheets gelatine
* 120ml (4fl oz) liquid glucose
* 1 tbsp glycerine
* 1kg (2¼lb) icing sugar, plus extra for dusting
* colouring paste

Tips

Pure extracts, oils, pastes, or powders (such as vanilla, almond oil, or cocoa powder) can flavour fondant. Knead in 1–2 drops of flavouring at a time, distributing evenly. Allow the fondant to rest in an airtight container for 30 minutes.

1 Soak the gelatine sheets in a bowl of cold water for about 10 minutes. Wring dry and stir into 60ml (2fl oz) warm water, one at a time, until dissolved. Mix in the glucose and glycerine until well blended, and set aside.

2 Sift the icing sugar into a large mixing bowl. Create a cavity in the centre and slowly pour in the liquid, a little at a time. Continue to stir, and mix until it forms a soft ball.

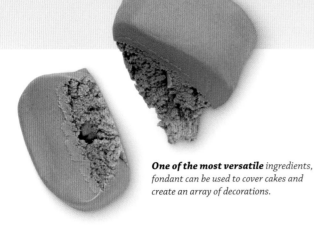

One of the most versatile *ingredients, fondant can be used to cover cakes and create an array of decorations.*

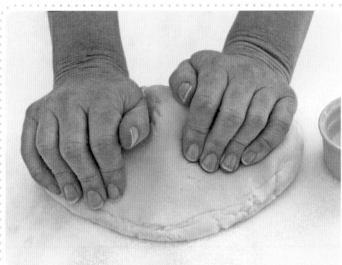

3 Dust a surface with icing sugar and tip the ball of fondant onto it. Knead it with your fingers until it is smooth and pliable, adding a little water if it is dry, or a little more icing sugar if it becomes tacky. When it reaches the desired consistency, roll it out and use it immediately, wrapping any leftovers in cling film for later use. Leave fondant-covered cakes to set and acquire a crust. Decorations dry hard, but can take up to a few days, depending on the humidity in your environment.

4 To colour the fondant, use a cocktail stick to apply a little colouring paste to the surface. Fold the fondant over the paste and then knead until it has a uniform colour throughout. For a marbled look, mix 1 or more colours of paste into fondant and knead it only partway through, just before you want to roll it out – creating a streaked effect. Kneading it again will cause the marbling to disappear.

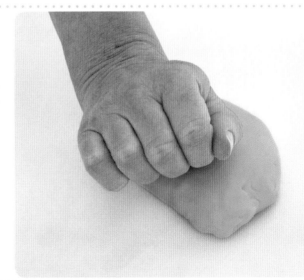

Fondant shapes *can be embossed with textured sheets and cutters (see pp104–05).*

Using embossing mats

This is an easy way to imprint fondant with texture, whether you are embossing the whole surface of a cake or decorations. You could, for example, create a leather texture on a handbag cake. Some mats have holes in them, allowing you to paint the surface of the fondant through them (rather like a stencil).

Equipment
* fondant roller
* embossing mat

Ingredients
* icing sugar, for dusting
* 1kg (2¼lb) fondant
* white vegetable fat, for greasing
* cake, crumb coated with buttercream icing

...an easy way to imprint fondant with texture

EMBOSSING WITH MATS
Carving and covering cakes **p65**
Building asymmetrical cakes **pp70–71**
Painting a colour wash **p146**

1 Dust a surface with icing sugar. Lightly grease the fondant roller and roll the fondant out to about 5mm (¼in) thick.

2 Grease the embossing mat and place it greased-side down onto the fondant. Roll evenly over the top of the mat.

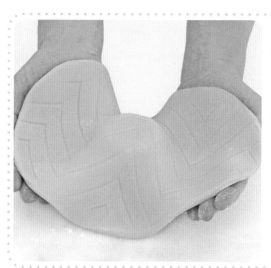

3 Remove the mat and lift the fondant over the top of the crumb-coated cake, using your hands to gently smooth it down without disrupting the pattern. You can also use this technique to emboss a covered cake drum (see p51).

Using embossing rollers

There is a wide range of different textured rollers that provide detail to the surface of fondant. Delicate patterns like this damask-style roller can transform cake coverings. You can also purchase "sleeves" that slip onto fondant rollers, which work in the same way.

Equipment
* fondant roller
* embossing roller

Ingredients
* icing sugar, for dusting
* 1kg (2¼lb) fondant
* white vegetable fat, for greasing

...provide detail to the surface of fondant

Tips
Buy embossing sticks to create patterns. These are ideal for smaller decorations or for cakes that are not fully embossed. Use white vegetable fat rather than icing sugar or cornflour, as these can cause cracking when pressed into the fondant.

1 Follow step 1, opposite, but roll out the fondant so it is just a little thicker. Carefully and lightly grease the embossing roller. You can also dust it with cornflour, but take care to brush off any excess to avoid disrupting the fine detailed pattern.

2 At the edge closest to you, press the roller into the fondant, and push it away from you, all the way to the other side. If you have a sheet of fondant that is wider than the roller, line up the roller so that it overlaps with the section that has already been embossed by about 3mm (⅛in). Keep the roller straight as you roll, applying even pressure.

Covering a cake

Apply fondant to levelled, filled cakes that have been crumb coated with buttercream or covered with marzipan. If you are covering a traditional fruitcake, brush the marzipan with a little water or brandy before you apply the fondant to ensure that it adheres. Smooth out the air bubbles as you cover the cake.

Equipment

* cake drum or board
* fondant roller
* fondant smoother

Ingredients

* icing sugar, for dusting
* 1kg (2¼lb) fondant
* 23cm (10in) 2-layer cake crumb coated with buttercream (see p29)

Smooth out the air bubbles as you cover the cake

Variation

Mini cakes are iced in the same way as large cakes; however, the fondant should be thin – for large cakes, roll it to about 4–5mm (⅙–¼in) thick; for mini cakes, it should be 2–3mm (¹⁄₁₆–⅛in) thick. For cupcakes, cut out circles to sit on top of the cakes.

1 Dust a surface with icing sugar. Knead and roll the fondant into a circle that can cover the cake with 5cm (2in) extra.

2 Unroll the fondant sheet onto the cake and smooth it across the top with a smoother, easing it down with your hands.

3 Trim off the excess fondant. Press the smoother evenly over the top of the cake and then run it down and around the sides of the cake, until perfectly smooth. To get a sharp edge at the top of the cake, you could use 2 smoothers at the same time, 1 on the top and the other on the sides, pressing them together at the edge.

Covering a cake drum

Cover cake drums in fondant, using matching or contrasting colours of your choice. You can emboss the fondant in the same way you would when covering a cake (see pp48–49), add stripes or other detail, and even paint or dust it. Always let it set overnight to firm up before you decorate further.

Equipment

* cake drum
* fondant roller
* fondant smoother

Ingredients

* icing sugar, for dusting
* tylose powder
* 1kg (2¼lb) fondant, strengthened (see p87)

1 Dust icing sugar on a surface and roll out the fondant into a circle 2mm (¹⁄₁₆in) thick and 30cm (12in) in diameter.

2 Mix together a pinch of tylose powder with 2 tablespoons of cold water until well blended and then brush over the cake drum.

...emboss the drum in the same way you would a cake

Tip

To avoid damaging the surface of the covered drum, place the cake on a board the exact size of the cake. Add a dab of edible glue or water to the centre of the board, and place the cake on top. You can use ribbon or piping to mask the join.

3 Carefully lift the fondant onto the drum and, using a smoother, smooth from the centre outwards to remove air bubbles. Press down around the sides and trim off any excess around the base of the drum with a sharp knife. Glue an edible or fabric ribbon around the circumference to finish.

Flower paste

Although traditionally used for fragile flowers, you can use flower paste to make any decorations you wish. It dries very hard, and even though it is technically edible, it is not normally eaten. You can colour it in the same way as you would with fondant.

 **PREP** 30 mins, plus thickening and chilling

 **MAKES** 500g (1lb 2oz)

Ingredients

* 2 tsp gelatine powder, dissolved in 5 tsp warm water and allowed to thicken for 30 minutes
* 2 tsp white vegetable fat
* 2 tsp liquid glucose
* 500g (1lb 2oz) icing sugar, sifted, plus extra for dusting
* 4 tsp tylose powder
* 1 egg white
* colouring paste, optional

Tips

Keep flower paste in an airtight container until ready to use. If the paste is sticky, work in a little more white vegetable fat until smooth and pliable. If it is too hard and crumbly, add a little more beaten egg white.

1 Place the thickened gelatine in a pan with the white vegetable fat and glucose. Stir over a low heat until the liquid is clear.

2 Transfer to the bowl of an electric whisk. Whisk in the icing sugar, tylose, and egg white. Turn it up to the highest setting.

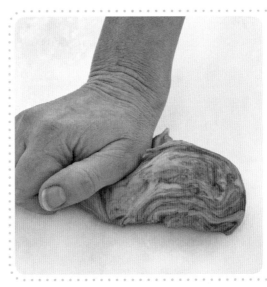

3 Continute to mix, until stringy and white. Refrigerate the mixture for 24–48 hours. Dust a surface with icing sugar and knead the mixture until it is smooth and pliable. Colour the paste, as shown with fondant on p47.

Mexican paste

This soft paste is ideal for cutting out shapes and modelling, as it does not stretch or lose its shape. Mexican paste is often used with tappits and patchwork cutters (see pp116–17). It takes a little time to incorporate the icing sugar, but its firm results are well worth the effort.

 **PREP** 30 mins, plus chilling

 **MAKES** 200g (7oz)

Ingredients

* 200g (7oz) icing sugar, sifted, plus extra for dusting
* 3 tsp tylose powder
* white vegetable fat, for greasing, optional
* colouring paste, optional

1 Stir the icing sugar and tylose powder in a bowl. Add 2 tablespoons of cold water and stir until the mixture holds together.

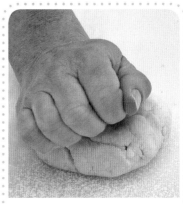

2 Place on a surface dusted with icing sugar. Knead firmly until you have a smooth ball. Do not add any more water.

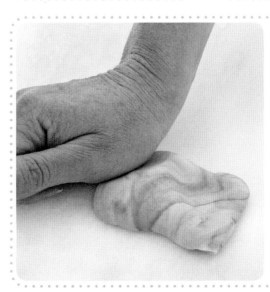

3 Wrap in cling film and refrigerate for 24 hours. Remove from the fridge and knead on a flat surface that is lightly dusted with icing sugar or greased with white vegetable fat, until smooth and pliable. You can colour the paste at this stage, or dust, spray, or paint it when your decorations are dry.

Tip

Avoid using cornflour to dust surfaces when preparing pastes as it will make the paste harder. Once the paste is ready, you can use cornflour to dust in the usual way, although white vegetable fat does produce better results with pastes.

DECORATING TECHNIQUES

Whether you want to decorate iced cakes with glitter butterflies, create exquisite sugar flower sprays, hand-model a pretty fondant princess, or pipe a three-layer cake, find every technique you need.

3D CREATIONS

Make your cakes truly spectacular and build strong foundations for your designs, by using 3D decorating techniques and a little imagination. Find out how to carve a cake into a novelty shape; create a model from rice treats; build durable shapes with gingerbread, fondant, or chocolate; and stack cakes into tiers with dowels and pillars.

Making a template

Templates are important for building easy and accurate 3D shapes. Draw around them to cut out the pieces of fondant, chocolate, or modelling paste that you need. You could draw on graph paper first, to help you with the proportions, or trace directly onto baking parchment.

Equipment
* graph paper
* cardboard

Create accurate and easy 3D shapes by tracing your own templates

1 Trace the outline of a shape you wish to duplicate, such as a shopping bag, onto graph paper. Tidy up the outline, using a ruler to make it symmetrical, if necessary. When you're happy with it, transfer the shape onto baking parchment and cut it out. Dust it with cornflour to prevent it from sticking to your medium.

2 To ensure that the template is accurate, cut the shapes from cardboard and glue them together as a trial run. You can also use this sample to support your creation as it dries.

Tip
Use hand-drawn or traced templates to sculpt slabs of cake into shapes, such as flowers with curved petals, Christmas trees, cartoon characters, or animals. Once you have a good outline, use the small, leftover chunks of cake as fillers for the shapes.

Using crisp rice shapes

Use crisp rice cereal to create decorative 3D designs. These are pliable and hold their shape well, allowing you to make intricate designs, which are often not possible with cake. For best results, refer to the object or a photograph of the object you are recreating.

Ingredients

* 50g (1¾oz) unsalted butter, softened
* 200g (7oz) miniature marshmallows
* ½ tsp vanilla extract
* 150g (5½oz) crisp rice cereal
* icing sugar, for dusting
* buttercream icing (see pp24–25)
* fondant, rolled to 5mm (¼in) thick

1 Melt the butter in a large pan over a medium heat and add the marshmallows. Cook for 3 minutes, stirring, until the marshmallows melt. Stir in the vanilla extract, remove from the heat, and add the cereal, mixing everything together. Transfer to a bowl and refrigerate until firm, about 1 hour.

2 Using a sharp knife, carve the basic shape of the model, and then work on finer details. If necessary, you can soften the crisp rice mixture any time by heating it for a few seconds in the microwave. This will make it more pliable, especially for moulding the smaller details.

Variation

You can use food-safe plastic, resin, rubber, or silicone moulds to create detailed shapes. Dust with a little cornflour or icing sugar, and then press the mixture firmly into the mould. Refrigerate until firm, ease out, and cover with fondant (step 6).

3 You can also dust your hands with icing sugar, warm the mixture slightly in your hands, and then mould it into shape. The firmer it is pressed, the more likely it is to hold its shape. Use cutters if necessary.

4 Mould details such as teddy bear ears, limbs, and other small parts with your hands and press them onto the model. If you need to, use cocktail sticks to keep them in place.

5 When the model is complete, refrigerate until firm (at least 1 hour). Gently warm a little buttercream icing to soften it, and brush over the model. This will help to fix the fondant in place.

6 Fold the fondant over the figure, pressing down gently. If you like, add pieces of fondant over the base layer to create details, moistening the back of each piece with water to adhere it.

Using chocolate moulds

Build 3D chocolate creations using large plastic moulds. There are several types of moulds, such as this piano, that allow you to assemble an entire 3D construction. Use dark, milk, or white chocolate, so long as it is correctly tempered (see pp40–41).

Equipment
* mould
* soft cotton gloves

Ingredients
* dark, milk, or white chocolate, melted and tempered (see pp40–41)

1 Polish the mould by wiping it with dry cotton wool. Lay it on a baking tray on a flat surface, propping up all the parts evenly.

2 Spoon the chocolate into the mould, and press it into the crevices with the back of a spoon. Tap it gently to release air bubbles.

Tips
Place the chocolate creation on top of a cake, or to its side, and keep in a cool room until ready to display. If there are any marks on the chocolate, spray it evenly with confectioner's spray glaze to produce a more uniform and shiny appearance.

3 Refrigerate the chocolate for about 20 minutes until set. Gently tap the mould to release the pieces onto baking parchment.

4 Wearing gloves, trim off any excess with a knife. Brush melted chocolate onto the pieces to join them. Allow to harden.

Cutting chocolate shapes

Use a template or hand-drawn pattern to cut shapes from a slab of hardened chocolate, and assemble a 3D construction, such as sides for a box. Use a very sharp, warm knife that cuts through the chocolate neatly, and work fast, as chocolate can melt quickly when handled.

Equipment

* food-grade acetate sheets
* cardboard or baking parchment templates

Ingredients

* white, dark, or milk chocolate, melted and tempered (see pp40–41)

…cut shapes from a slab of hardened chocolate

Variation

You can create curved 3D surfaces by placing another acetate sheet on top of the chocolate slab. When it begins to harden but is still pliable, carefully wrap it around a bowl or can. This will help to support its weight and create a curved shape.

1 Line a baking tray with a food-grade acetate sheet. Cut out templates (see p57) from baking parchment.

2 Spread the melted, tempered chocolate over the acetate with a palette knife to the desired thickness. Chill for 15 minutes.

3 Trace the templates with a knife, cutting through most of the surface. Return to the fridge and chill until hard.

4 Heat a sharp knife in hot water, wipe dry, and cut through to the base of the shapes. Assemble as described opposite.

Building with fondant

Create buildings, bricks, and other 3D shapes such as this boat, by using fondant strengthened with tylose powder (see p87). Use a template to design your 3D creation, moulding fondant to form any shape and letting it dry on supports. Fix the pieces together with edible glue.

Equipment

* cardboard or baking parchment templates
* cardboard or cardboard box, for supports

Ingredients

* cornflour, for dusting
* strengthened fondant (see p87)
* edible glue

Mould fondant to form any shape you like

Tips

For tall creations, insert a cake-pop stick, a wooden skewer, or a food-safe wire into the fondant to provide support. Strengthened fondant dries out quickly, so work on small portions at a time, keeping the remainder covered in cling film.

1 Dust a surface with cornflour and roll out the fondant to the desired thickness. Roll it thickly if it needs to support other pieces.

2 Cut the desired shape using a template (see p57) or a ruler. Make sure you cut a base to support the creation.

3 Dry for 2–3 days on baking parchment, until firm. For arched shapes, place pieces on a curved, cornflour-dusted surface.

4 Pipe, paint, or draw details onto dry shapes before you join them, taking care not to smudge them as you do so.

5 Using a small, clean paintbrush, join the shapes together with edible glue, or by simply moistening the sides with water and holding them firmly in place until they stick.

Variation

Press the strengthened fondant into moulds (such as building blocks or other shapes; see pp120–23) and, once dry, stack or layer them to create a 3D construction. Work carefully with more delicate designs as they have a tendency to break easily.

6 It is a good idea to provide some support inside the creation until the glue dries. Use a small cardboard box to support a design such as this boat. You could place a box or a cylinder inside a fondant building or a turret to give added support.

Creating strong 3D objects

For complex modelling paste objects, such as this shoe, use cardboard or baking parchment templates to ensure accuracy. Choose a sturdy paste, such as flower or Mexican paste, and provide adequate support for the shapes as they dry, so that they maintain their 3D quality.

Equipment

* cardboard or baking parchment templates
* cardboard box, for support

Ingredients

* sheet of flower paste, or other modelling paste
* cornflour, for dusting
* edible glue

Tip

While the paste is still slightly pliable, emboss the surface with modelling tools or cutters, pressed just into the paste but not through it. This is a good way to make a shoe label, for instance. Decorate after the glue has fully dried.

1 To make a shoe, roll the paste on a cornflour-dusted surface. Roll a thick piece for the sole. Use a knife to cut around the template.

2 Create a support for the shape. For a high-heeled shoe, use a cardboard box covered in cling film for support.

3 Make supports for each part, and leave to dry overnight. When nearly dry, check the shape and adjust, if needed.

4 To form the shoe, paint edible glue on the edges and press them together. Allow each part to dry before moving on to the next.

Carving and covering cakes

Carve cakes to create 3D replicas of almost anything, from handbags and trains, to cars and guitars (see below). Choose a firm, dense cake, such as Madeira, which will hold its shape and support the weight of the icing. Be sure the cake has cooled before you freeze it.

Equipment

* cardboard or baking parchment templates

Ingredients

* buttercream icing (see pp24–25)
* round or square Madeira cake, depending on the shape of your design (see p231)
* fondant, rolled to 5mm (¼in) thick

Tip
Every carved cake needs a basic layer of fondant wrapped around it, as shown in step 3. Once this has rested and formed a crust, you can add further layers of fondant in different colours, as well as detail and other decorations.

1 Spread buttercream icing between the layers of your cake, and freeze for 30 minutes. For tall designs, thin layers work better.

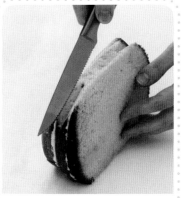

2 Use a very sharp knife to carve the cake into the basic shape you want. Then use a small, sharp knife for detailing.

3 Let the cake rest for an hour. Crumb coat with buttercream icing (see p29), then cover with fondant. Press it into the crevices.

For 2D shapes, use a very sharp knife to cut carefully around a template. Neaten the edges and then proceed with step 3.

Building with gingerbread

The secret to a successful gingerbread construction is good-quality dough, a symmetrically drawn template, and precise baking time. You will also need patience, as you must wait for the glue or royal icing fixative to dry as you construct, to ensure a sturdy finished product.

Equipment

* cardboard or baking parchment templates

Ingredients

* gingerbread dough (see p235), rolled to 5mm (¼in) thick
* royal icing, for piping (see p35)

Variations

You can create trees, towers, windmills, and fairy bowers with gingerbread. For cylindrical shapes, wrap the gingerbread pieces around a can while they are warm. If you are unsure whether the construction will work, do a trial run with cardboard and glue.

1 To create a house, lay the templates on the gingerbread dough. Use a sharp knife to cut around the templates neatly.

2 Using a palette knife, move the dough pieces onto a baking tray lined with baking parchment, ensuring they lie flat.

3 Bake according to the recipe instructions. Trim any rough edges with a sharp, hot knife, and leave the pieces to cool.

4 Once cool, pipe your designs on the cooled gingerbread pieces before you assemble your creation, if desired.

Once dry, pipe the roof with royal icing to create snow and icicles, or simply decorate to taste

Use thin layers of icing to stick the pieces together, allowing each layer to dry before adding another

5 To assemble, work from the bottom upwards, applying royal icing or sugar glue (see p235) to the joins with a palette knife.

6 Allow each join to dry. Ensure the base is dry before you attach the roof. Hold the pitched roof in place for a few minutes.

Tips
Always assemble the gingerbread construction on the board on which it will be presented. Moving it later could cause pieces to shift. Colour your royal icing with colouring paste for specific shades or to make the piping stand out.

Building tiered cakes

Stack a light iced sponge cake directly onto the cake below it without support. For dense cakes covered in fondant or any cake structure taller than two layers (as shown here), you will need dowels and cake boards to keep the structure steady and prevent it from collapsing.

Equipment

* cake boards, in varying sizes, to suit size of your cakes
* dowels
* wire cutters

Ingredients

* fondant-covered or iced cakes in varying sizes, according to your design
* icing sugar, for dusting
* royal icing, for sticking

Variation

Use a long dowel and embed it through all the cake tiers from top to bottom. This will keep the structure steady and prevent movement. Cut circles from the centre of each board in advance, to make it easier for the dowel to run through.

1 Dust the base cake with icing sugar. Position a board the same size as the small cake on top. Press down gently to leave a guideline.

2 Insert a dowel into the cake. Nick it with a knife at the height of the cake. Cut all dowels to the same height with wire cutters.

3 Insert the dowels into the cake, straight down until they touch the board. Space them 2.5cm (1in) in from the guideline.

4 Carefully centre and then fix the small cake and its board on top with a little royal icing. Repeat the process for more tiers.

Building with pillars

If you want to use solid pillars, simply dowel the cake (see opposite), positioning the dowels where you want the pillars to be. Place the pillars on top of the dowels, securing them to the cake and to the cake board above, with royal icing. For hollow pillars, follow this step-by-step.

Equipment

* dowels
* 6 pillars
* wire cutters
* cake boards, in varying sizes, to suit size of your cakes
* piping bag with small, round tip, optional

Ingredients

* fondant-covered or iced cakes in varying sizes, according to your design
* icing sugar, for dusting
* royal icing, for sticking

Tip

An easy and reliable way to construct a tiered cake is to use a specialized stand – cakes sit on plates that fit directly into it. You can also use interlocking separators that fit over a central post, thus perfectly centering the tiers and supporting them.

1 Place the dowels where you want the pillars to sit – evenly spaced around the cake. Mark the cake with the position of each.

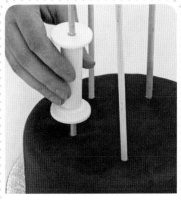

2 Place a dowel into each mark, pushing it through the cake until it hits the board beneath. Slide the pillar over the top.

3 Using wire cutters, cut the dowel so it is the exact height of the top of the pillar. Cut the other dowels to the same height.

4 Pipe or spread royal icing to the top and base of each pillar, slide them onto the dowels, and place the cake and board on top.

Building asymmetrical cakes

Asymmetrical cakes are not only visually stunning but are also relatively easy to make, so long as you use a firm, dense cake (such as Madeira) and a dowel in the centre for support. Begin by partially freezing each cake on its board, as this makes them easier to carve.

Equipment

* 1 cake board, for the base
* 2 or more cake boards, the size of your cake tiers, with a hole the width of the dowel pierced through their centre
* long wooden dowel, sharpened at one end
* shorter dowels (see p68)
* wire cutters

Ingredients

* 2 or more Madeira cakes (see p231), in varying sizes, according to your design; levelled and layered with buttercream
* buttercream icing (see pp24–25)
* cornflour, for dusting
* fondant

1 Carve the cakes when they are almost frozen. Carve the top of the base tier at an angle so it slopes at a diagonal level.

2 Position the next tier on top. Hold it firmly with one hand, and use a knife to score the top of the cake at an opposite diagonal.

3 Check the layers are even. Repeat to add more tiers. Use the tier beneath for support as you cut.

4 When the cakes are all cut with angled tops, crumb coat each cake (see p29) and chill between ½ hour–1 hour.

5 Dust a surface with cornflour and roll out a large piece of fondant. Carefully lift it over the top of the bottom tier, smoothing downwards to cover it (see p50). Repeat with all the tiers, until each one is fully covered.

6 To stack the cakes, insert dowels (see p68) in all of the tiers except the top one. Cut each dowel using wire cutters to make sure that it sits flush with the top of each angled cake.

7 Dot a little buttercream icing in the centre of each tier and stack 1 on top of the other, ensuring they are centred – the long dowel needs to run smoothly through the cakes and the holes in their boards.

8 Carefully press the long dowel through all the tiers until it hits the cake board of the base tier. Cut it so that it is exactly the same height as the uppermost tier. Add a decoration to disguise it.

PIPING

Master the art of piping and elevate your cakes from simple to sensational. Start by learning how to make and fill a piping bag and practise the techniques – soon you'll create intricate piping with ease. Pipe flowers, foliage, borders, lettering, embroidery, beading, stringwork, and other decorative touches, using a variety of piping tips and ingredients.

Making a piping bag

Make a piping bag yourself using a square piece of baking parchment or greaseproof paper. Fill it with small quantities of piping mediums, and pipe fine lines and effects easily. Snip the end and pipe without a tip, or add a tip of your choice (see p20) with or without a coupler.

Equipment

* baking parchment or greaseproof paper
* masking tape

Simply snip the end and pipe with small quantities of icing

1 Fold the lower corner of the baking parchment upwards so that it is folded in half diagonally. Run your finger along the fold.

2 Fold over the whole of the top folded section without creasing it, rolling it over until you have a cone shape.

3 Fold the bottom folded section around the outside. Using your hand, expand it out, and then secure the shape with a little masking tape. Cut off any excess paper from the top.

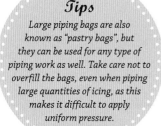

Tips

Large piping bags are also known as "pastry bags", but they can be used for any type of piping work as well. Take care not to overfill the bags, even when piping large quantities of icing, as this makes it difficult to apply uniform pressure.

Filling a piping bag

A piping bag should be densely packed with filling, but only at the tip end – don't overfill it. Squeeze the icing towards the tip, removing any air bubbles. Use any one of the huge variety of tips available to create a multitude of decorative touches on cakes and cupcakes.

Equipment

* piping bag with tips
* coupler, optional
* scraper, optional

Ingredients

* royal icing, for piping (see p35)

Squeeze the icing towards the tip, removing any air bubbles

Tip

Couplers are devices that allow you to change tips without emptying or refilling the piping bag. A base piece is placed inside the bottom of the bag, a tip is fitted into the screw-on top, and the top and tip are then screwed onto the base.

1 Fit the tip to the piping bag, with a coupler, if desired, and place it upright in a tall glass. Spoon in the buttercream icing.

2 Remove the bag from the glass and squeeze it towards the tip. Lay on a surface and press towards the tip, using a scraper, if desired.

3 Lift up the piping bag and twist the excess bag at the top, to ensure that the icing is tightly wrapped. Pipe as usual (see opposite).

Basic royal icing piping

Learn how to apply pressure to the piping bag correctly and increase your piping confidence. Create small or large decorative touches by controlling the flow with firm or light pressure. Stop the pressure completely and lift the tip away at the end of each design.

Equipment

✽ piping bag with tip

Ingredients

✽ royal icing, for piping (see p35)
✽ fondant-covered or iced cake

Control the flow with firm or light pressure

Tip

The consistency of icing is very important. Make sure the royal icing is firm but not runny. If it is too hard, the lines will break, curl, or crumble; too soft and they will run. See p35 for details about the right consistency for piping.

1 Fill the piping bag with royal icing, as shown opposite. Hold the bag in your right hand (or left, if you are left-handed), between your thumb and first 2 fingers. Hold the bag steady with your other hand. When the tip touches the surface of the cake, gently squeeze the icing out.

2 Even pressure is crucial. Too little pressure will produce scrawny lines, while too much will make piping difficult to control. Let the icing catch the surface and then gently lift the tip away from the surface, letting the icing fall. At the end of the line, stop the pressure and lift the tip away.

Piping with buttercream icing

Much softer than royal icing, pipe buttercream with any tip and in any colour to create a wide variety of decorative effects on iced cakes or cake drums. It's perfect for cupcakes, too. Varying the size of the tip and the pressure you apply can change the design dramatically.

Shell border
Use a medium open star tip for a shell border. Allow the icing to fan out as you drag and drop.

Zigzag border
An open star tip can create an attractive pattern that works well on the surface of cakes.

Swirl border
Use an open star tip to create a series of interlinked, scroll-like swirls.

Dot border
Create a row of symmetrical dots or beads with a medium round tip.

Stars and star border
Create individual stars (below) or link them together as a border, using a medium open star tip.

Piped leaves

Use a small leaf tip to create leaves, ruffling the lengths and dragging the piped icing to a tip.

Basketweave

A medium basketweave tip is used here, with small sections of piping in a woven pattern over longer lines of buttercream.

Grass

Short strands of grass (and even fur or hair) can be created with a small multi-opening grass tip.

Longer grass

Pipe longer, wider strands of buttercream with a medium multi-opening grass tip to create grass and individual hair strands.

Rosette border

Use a medium open star tip to swirl tiny rosettes that can be linked or used individually.

Pulled bead border

Use a medium round tip to pipe beads and then slowly release the pressure as you drag each bead.

C-scroll border

Linking up a series of "C"s, using a small open star tip, creates an easy and pretty border; alternate "C"s with "S"s for a different look.

Rope border

Create a sturdy rope or a series of scrolls by linking a series of backwards "S"s with a medium open star tip.

Ruffle border

Pipe a simple ruffled border using a medium petal tip, dragging the icing back on itself and then forward again.

Piping buttercream borders

Buttercream is an excellent medium for piping decorative borders or effects. You can pipe figures, flowers, and other decorations, and even use it for brushwork embroidery (see p139). Get the consistency of the buttercream right (see p24), and use the correct tips.

Equipment

* piping bag fitted with an open star tip (such as Wilton no. 21), filled with buttercream icing (see pp24–25)

Ingredients

* round smooth-iced cake on a fondant-covered cake drum

Buttercream is excellent for piping borders or effects

Tip

If the buttercream has air bubbles after beating, press them out against the sides of the bowl with a spatula to help you to get a smooth product. Avoid overfilling the bag, as it will warm in your hands and the icing will melt.

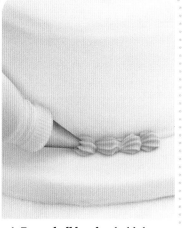

1 **For a shell border**, hold the bag at a 45° angle just above the cake surface. Squeeze, so that the icing fans out.

2 Relax the pressure, and pull the bag along the base of the cake. Pull the tip along to form a point. Repeat.

For drop flowers, hold the bag directly above the cake surface, just touching. Squeeze, letting the icing build up to make a flower. Stop squeezing and lift the tip away. You could turn the hand that is holding the bag as you squeeze out the icing for a swirl, and/or add a dragée to the centre.

Piping a buttercream rose

Pipe a simple rose using buttercream icing. It can be piped directly onto a small square of baking parchment, onto a cake in a single, flowing movement (see Variation), or piped onto a flower nail, as shown here, and then applied to the cake when the buttercream has firmed a little.

Equipment

* piping bag, fitted with a coupler and a round tip (such as Wilton no. 12), filled with buttercream icing (see pp24–25)
* petal tip (such as Wilton no. 104)
* flower nail

1 Hold the tip above the centre of the flower nail. Apply pressure and squeeze out a cone shape of icing.

2 Change to a petal tip. Hold the bag at a 45° angle and squeeze to form a ribbon of icing that overlaps at the top of the cone.

Variation

To pipe a buttercream rose with a single movement, attach a large or medium open star tip to your piping bag. Pipe a dab of buttercream to create a centre, and then carefully work your way around the centre in an anticlockwise motion to create a swirl.

3 Place the wide end of the tip against the base of the bud. Squeeze and move the tip up and then down to the base. Repeat for 3 petals around the bud, overlapping each petal just behind the edge of the first. Repeat the same technique, creating a row of 5 petals and finally a row of 7, angling the tip to create an open rose.

Piping dots, beads, and flowers

Decorate the top of a cupcake with a series of simple piped royal icing picot dots, beads, and flowers. Picot is a type of elegant "embroidery" that can be undertaken with a series of small, simply piped dots. For a different effect that is as easy to achieve, try a beaded border.

Equipment
* piping bag fitted with a small, round tip (such as Wilton no. 1L), filled with piping-consistency royal icing (see p35)

Ingredients
* fondant-covered or royal-iced cake

For picot dots, hold the bag so the tip is just above the cake. Pipe a dot, increasing pressure to increase its size. Stop squeezing to drop it.

For beads, hold the bag at a 45° angle. Apply pressure as you lift to allow the icing to spread out. Stop the pressure as you drop it.

Tip
When piping picot dots, do not gradually stop the pressure, or you will get a "nose" on the dot. Instead, stop squeezing and pull away immediately. Allow to dry just slightly, dip your finger in a little cornflour, and gently press it down.

For flowers, prepare the bag as before. Pipe a small dot and then push the point of the tip into the edge and drag it towards you in a petal shape. Continue, piping another dot beside the first one, working in a circle, until you form a flower.

Piping filigree with royal icing

Using a series of interlinked "W"s and "M"s, or simply long, continuous curls and lines, filigree is an elegant piping technique that you can use to create delicate, lace-like designs. Similar in approach, scrolled hearts can be piped on baking parchment and attached to the cake once dry.

Equipment

* piping bag fitted with a small, very fine round tip (such as PME 00 or 0), filled with piping-consistency royal icing (see p35)
* template, optional

Ingredients

* fondant-covered or royal-iced cake or cupcake
* edible glue

Tips

For more intricate designs, you can use an icing "pen", which you fill with icing and use with one hand. The pen pushes the icing out without the need to squeeze. You can also purchase icing syringes, onto which you fit specialized tips.

1 Pipe an outline with the tip positioned just above the surface of the cake. Apply uniform, gentle pressure.

2 Pipe curves, bending continuously in all directions, but never touching. Do not lift the tip from the surface.

For scrolled hearts, use a template, if desired, to pipe a design onto a sheet of baking parchment. Dry until hard (overnight, if possible), carefully remove from the parchment, and affix them around the sides of your cake with a little edible glue.

Piping with royal icing

Create elegant and detailed designs with royal icing, which can dry hard and hold its shape for 2D and 3D work. Colour as desired and use with dozens of different tips for varied effects. Piping is a skill really worth mastering, to achieve a truly professional finish.

Scrolls

Use a small shell or rope tip to create a series of interlinked scrolls for a border on a cake.

Rope

Use a rope tip to pipe a spring shape in a clockwise direction, using even pressure.

Filigree

This delicate piping work is created with a small writing tip and long piped lines of random patterns. Dust with lustre dust to highlight.

Beads and stringwork

Try small and large writing tips to create a finely piped line of beads. Link with loops of piped string work.

Shells and stringwork

Use a shell tip to create a row of symmetrical shapes, and then link them with piped stringwork, finishing off with a picot dot at the base of each shell.

Ruffles and rosettes

A star tip creates a lovely rosette when turned in a clockwise motion. Link with a series of ruffles, using a small petal or open-star tip, and embellish with stringwork.

Shell border with stringwork

Use a shell tip to create a continuous shell border, and then a writing nozzle to pipe in diagonal lines for a lattice beneath.

Star border

Create a star border in any size, with an open-star tip. Apply pressure until you get the required size, and then lift the bag upright for each shape.

Pulled beadwork

Use a slightly larger writing tip to create soft beads of icing and then drag them across to form a thinner tail.

Skein border

A skein is created with a small star tip, by piping in a clockwise direction at an even height to form the first curve and then pulling down in a point.

Zigzag ruffles

Use a small open star tip and pipe in a delicate back-and-forth motion to create the appearance of ruffles.

Swirls and picot dots

Use a fine writing tip to create elegantly piped curls, surrounding the larger swirls with a series of picot dots.

Damask 1

This ornate design can be created using a fine writing nozzle to pipe over a template or in the cut-out sections of a stencil.

Damask 2

To create this delicate pattern on the side of a cake, press a template onto the surface of the fondant and use a veining tool to emboss the shape for piping.

Trailing branches

Create fine and then slightly wider lines with a fine writing tip, and use the same tip for the beaded blossoms on the branches.

Piping lettering

Piped lettering is one of the trickiest skills to learn, but if you master the technique you will be able to add a professional touch to your cake. The secret of successful piping is patience and practice. Pipe on baking parchment, then freeze until hard, or pipe directly on your cake.

Equipment

* tracing paper or baking parchment template, optional
* piping bag with a small, round decorating tip (Wilton no. 1L)

Ingredients

* royal icing, for piping (see p35) or thinned buttercream (see p24)
* fondant-covered or royal-iced cake

Tips

Use royal icing to pipe onto fondant-covered cakes and use buttercream icing for buttercream-iced cakes. Use more pressure for heavier lines (down strokes, when you are writing in script) and less pressure for thinner lines (upstrokes).

1 Place your template (if using) on the cake and use a cocktail stick to mark out the letters. Fill the piping bag with icing.

2 Place the tip just above the surface of the cake, with the bag at a 45° angle, and begin piping.

3 Apply pressure and drag the tip along the surface, as you form the letters. Release the pressure to end a line.

For block letters, apply pressure, lift, and move along the line of the letter. Release pressure with the tip pressed onto the surface.

Piping with chocolate

You can pipe chocolate onto the surface of a cake, or allow the designs to harden in the fridge on a sheet of baking parchment, ready to affix later. Chocolate should be lukewarm to pipe effectively. Temper the chocolate (see pp40–41) for the shiniest and hardest results.

Equipment

* tracing paper or baking parchment template, optional
* piping bag with small, round decorating tip (such as Wilton no. 1L)

Ingredients

* milk, white, or dark chocolate, melted and tempered (see pp40–41)

1 Fill the piping bag with melted and tempered milk chocolate that has slightly cooled, so it is just warm. Fix a sheet of baking parchment on top of the template, and fix the sides with paper clips to hold it steady.

2 Press the tip against the surface of the baking parchment at the centre of the design and, working from the inside out, pipe lines over the template. Drag the tip along the paper, leaving a neat line of piping. Stop the pressure at the end of each line, and repeat, piping each line separately. Chill until hard.

HAND-MODELLING

Work malleable mediums such as fondant and flower paste by hand to produce beautiful decorations that enhance your cakes. Make delightful 3D models, such as realistic flowers and leaves, or characters for novelty cakes, with the help of the right tools and these impressive techniques.

Strengthening fondant

Whether you choose to model fondant entirely by hand, or use cutters to create a variety of shapes, it is important to prepare the fondant so that it is pliable, strong, and able to dry hard enough. Use small quantities at a time, leaving the rest double-wrapped in cling film.

Ingredients

* white vegetable fat, for greasing
* 500g (1lb 2oz) fondant
* 2 tsp tylose powder

...pliable, strong, and able to dry hard enough for cutting and modelling

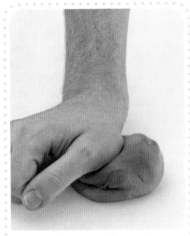

1 Lightly grease a flat surface and place the fondant on top. Knead the fondant until it is smooth. Make a well in the centre.

2 Place the tylose powder inside. Press the fondant around the well and knead the ingredients together.

Tips

Always use "flower" grade or finely milled tylose powder to strengthen fondant. Coarser-milled powders are fine for making edible glue, but will make fondant lumpy and cause it to harden unevenly. Strengthen after colouring fondant, not before.

3 When the fondant is smooth, pliable, and evenly coloured (with no streaks of strengthening powder), double-wrap it in cling film and place in a zip-lock bag to rest for 2 hours or overnight. You can omit this resting time, but it may lose some of its elasticity.

Modelling a fondant rose

You can easily mould impressive, blooming roses using your fingers and a ball tool, as shown here. To save time and create an even shape, you could cut out the petals using petal cutters in a mix of three or four sizes. This technique works well with chocolate modelling clay, too.

Equipment

* 18-gauge florist's wire
* ball tool

Ingredients

* 25g (scant 1oz) fondant, strengthened (see p87)
* white vegetable fat, for greasing

Mould impressive, blooming roses

Tips

Knead in a little more tylose powder or gum tragacanth when modelling the cones, so that they require less drying time. It is possible to create a rose on an undried cone, but it may not hold its shape as successfully.

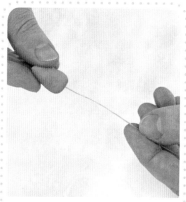

1 Form a cone of fondant on the wire. Place upright to harden for 3 days. When dry, grease your surface and roll a ball of fondant.

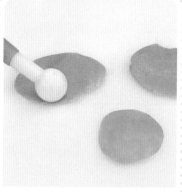

2 Press out into a small oval, 1mm (1/16in) thick. Create 5 more and cover with cling film. Use a ball tool to soften the edges.

3 Moisten the base of each petal with a little water and attach to the cone, overlapping each petal to form a tight bud.

4 Repeat, moulding larger petals. Add around 20 petals, using larger petals to form an open rose. Place on a stand to dry overnight.

Modelling a simple tulip

Tulips are easy to make and, unlike roses, require only one cutter. Use a calyx cutter for the base, or form a star with your fingers. Alternatively, you could hand-model the petals as you would for the rose (see opposite), with one end of the oval slightly narrower than the other.

Equipment

* ❋ fondant roller
* ❋ petal cutter
* ❋ scriber tool
* ❋ calyx cutter

Ingredients

* ❋ white vegetable fat, for greasing
* ❋ 25g (scant 1oz) fondant, strengthened (see p87), rolled to 2mm (1/16in) thick
* ❋ 12g (1/2oz) green fondant, strengthened (see p87)

1 On a greased surface, roll a tiny ball of fondant. Cut out 3 petals using the cutter. Draw down the centre of each, using a scriber tool.

2 Moisten the base of a petal, and press it around the ball. Repeat with all petals. Overlap them for an open tulip.

3 Roll out the green fondant, and cut a calyx with the cutter. Moisten and press onto the base of the tulip. If desired, you can press the petals closed at the top with your fingers.

Variations

To create frilled petals for the tulip, make tiny cuts around the petal outline, then roll a frilling tool over the edge of each petal. To make your own inedible stamens, use thick thread that has been stiffened with edible glue, attaching a tiny ball of fondant at the tip.

Creating flowers and sprays

Cut and vein realistic flowers from fondant or flower paste, tint them with petal dust, and then wire them together for dramatic sprays (see pp112–13). There is a wealth of cutters that can produce many types of flowers. They provide the perfect finishing touch to any celebration cake.

Purple roses

Wire simple fondant roses in vibrant colours into sprays for dramatic effect.

Poinsettia

Cut out petals and leaves in a range of sizes, vein them with a veining mat, and layer to create a gorgeous Christmas blossom.

Orchids, cornflowers, and baby's breath

Create a trailing spray by wiring together larger flowers at one end and smaller ones at the other, filling spaces with small blossoms and leaves.

Calla spray

A simple spray of uniform-sized lilies is easy to wire with veined green foliage and makes a stunning and effective centrepiece.

Orchid spray

Wire together an orchid, cut from thinly rolled paste and tinted with dust, with foliage and blossoms. Use a sharp knife to vein the leaves.

Freesia

Colour fondant lilac, and create a spray of freesia, wrapping together the blooms with florist's tape (see pp112–13).

Cornflowers

Use specialist cutters for vivid blue cornflowers. Using a garlic press, create strands of paste that can be rolled into shape for the central stamens.

Cymbidium orchid

Stipple the inside of the bell with a stiff brush and a little petal dust mixed with rejuvenator spirit or vodka. Ruffle the veined bell with a frilling tool.

Gerbera and freesia

A daisy or gerbera plunger cutter will emboss the surface of the petals. Layer and wire with freesia and blossoms.

Jasmine

Try using a calyx cutter for jasmine. Lightly tint the centres of jasmine blossoms with pink petal dust to highlight the veining on the petals.

Lilies

Wrap teardrops of white paste around sturdy yellow stamens. Score the leaves and petals for realism.

Freesia trailing spray

Wiring together single leaves on a central wire creates a trailing spray. Bright freesia with white stamens are accompanied by individually wired white blossoms.

Rose spray

Use a little brown petal dust on flower-paste leaves, and then steam to provide a soft sheen. Attach to rose buds in various sizes.

Orchid

Create the petals and centre of an orchid with a specialist cutter and a veining tool. Try using darker petal dust on the outside edges, softening the shade towards the centre.

Modelling a basic figure

With some careful modelling and sculpting, you can make figures like this little girl. You can use a veining tool to add creases to fabric, or a frilling tool to form curls in the strands of fondant hair, if desired. You could even adapt her to become a princess (see pp170–75).

Equipment

* cake-pop stick, halved
* stitching (quilting) tool
* veining tool
* scalpel
* cocktail stick
* fondant roller
* small blossom cutter
* garlic press

Ingredients

* 100g (3½oz) each of lilac and pale pink fondant, strengthened (see p87)
* 50g (1¾oz) fondant for the head and body, strengthened (see p87)
* black edible felt-tip pen
* pink edible felt-tip pen
* pink lustre dust
* cornflour, for dusting
* 1 tsp yellow fondant, strengthened (see p87)
* 25g (1oz) fondant for the hair, strengthened (see p87)
* edible glue

1 Form a large ball of kneaded fondant into a teardrop shape. Flatten the top and base, and smooth it down so that the base fans out. Insert the cake-pop stick through the centre. Shape a smaller ball of lilac fondant into a bodice shape. Slip it onto the stick and add detail with a stitching tool. Use a veining tool to score folds.

2 Model 2 narrow cones of pale pink fondant that are curved at each end, with one end wider than the other. Use the veining tool to score creases into the sleeves, and bend the arms at the elbow. Allow to harden for 30 minutes, and then moisten with a little water and fix to the top of the bodice.

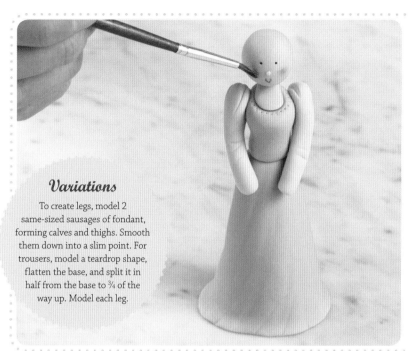

Variations

To create legs, model 2 same-sized sausages of fondant, forming calves and thighs. Smooth them down into a slim point. For trousers, model a teardrop shape, flatten the base, and split it in half from the base to ¾ of the way up. Model each leg.

3 To make the neck, knead fondant into a neat oval that fits into the neckline of the dress, moisten the base, and slide it onto the stick. Smooth it down into the bodice and use your fingers to shape the neck. Allow to dry for 30 minutes while you make the head. Form an egg-shaped ball of fondant into a head, with a gentle curve for the chin and a tiny oval for the nose. Mark the eyes with the fine black edible pen and draw in the mouth with the pink pen. Brush the cheeks with a little pink lustre dust and slide the head onto the stick.

4 Cut a thin strip of pink fondant and fix it to the waist. Cut 2 more strips and fix to the front of the skirt for a sash. Create hands by shaping fondant into 2 tiny teardrops. Use a scalpel to cut 4 fingers and a thumb on each hand, and then add shape using a cocktail stick. Poke a small hole into the wrist of each arm and attach the hands to the sleeves. Draw one over the other and fix with a little water. Roll out the strengthened yellow fondant on a cornflour-dusted surface and cut a blossom with the cutter. Fix it to the bodice. Press balls of fondant through a garlic press to create hair. Glue the strands onto the head with edible glue so that the sections meet at a side parting.

Modelling characters

Colour and model strengthened fondant, modelling pastes, or clays to create delightful characters for your cakes. You can embellish them with the use of basic tools, piping, edible paints, dusts, and pens ... and a little imagination.

Ballerina
Try a garlic press for natural-looking hair and a frilling tool for her skirt. It's easy to paint the laces for the ballet shoes.

Ladybird
Use a large round piping tip to cut black fondant dots, and flower stamens for the antennae.

Mouse
You can pipe or purchase googly eyes, and then score a thin rectangle of flower paste for the teeth.

Rabbit
Create the body in a single colour and add the features afterwards, scoring the cheeks with a frilling tool.

Fairy
Rice paper, cut to shape, makes delicate wings. Try marbling the base of the toadstool.

Cat
Flower stamens make great whiskers. Scoring the fondant creates the furry stripes.

Dog
Try using veining and frilling tools and pieces of fondant to add detail to the face and body.

Chicken
Fondant wings can be scored into feathers with the back of a knife.

Elf
Give his clothing a realistic touch by pleating the fondant and scoring in folds with a veining tool.

Sheep

Try using a frilling tool to create the white fondant fleece. Leave it to dry before adding the black details.

Baby ladybird

Use a circle of thin white flower paste or rice paper for the eyes, and colour in the pupils with a black edible pen.

Pirate

Use stitching and veining tools to emboss the clothing, and give his beard a realistic touch.

Cow

This cow has modelled legs on a basic tear-shaped body, and individual shaped spots.

Dragonfly

Carefully score a fondant body with a thin knife or scalpel and adorn with rice paper wings.

Teddy

Use a blade or stitching tool to add seams, and pipe a dot of black icing onto thin fondant circles for his eyes.

Pig

A basic tear shape can form the body of a pig, or a number of different creatures.

Elephant

It is all in the detail! Gently scored lines produce a lovely weathered hide. Model the trunk and head in one piece and then add ears.

Football player

Try making his body first and then "dressing him" with thinly rolled fondant shapes.

Westie

Create his fur with a veining tool and by simply pulling bits of the fondant into points.

Modelling embellishments

You can adorn cakes or decorations with swags, bows, ruffles, ropes, and chains. These techniques take a little time to master, but they add beautiful detail to your creations. Use a stitching tool to quilt the edges of the swags before you pleat them, for prettier bows.

Equipment
* fondant roller
* veining tool
* circular cutters, 1 large and 1 small
* flower mat or foam
* frilling tool

Ingredients
* strengthened fondant (see p87)
* cornflour, for dusting

Add beautiful detail to your creations

Tips
Paint your chains (see opposite) with metallic lustre dust mixed with rejuvenator spirit one side at a time, allowing the paint to dry fully before turning over and painting the other side. You could also airbrush the links to create texture.

1 **For a swag**, roll out a small rectangle of fondant on a cornflour-dusted surface, cut to neaten the edges, and pleat folds.

2 Gather up the fondant on each side, and pinch it together at the top, moistening it with a little water. Cut off any excess.

1 **For a bow**, create 2 swags. Fold them over so the pinched edges meet. Model a smaller rectangular swag for the centre.

2 Fix with water. Wrap the centre swag around the join and fix together at the back. Use a veining tool to neaten the pleats.

1 **For ruffles**, roll out a thin square of fondant on a dusted surface and use a cutter to cut out a large circle. Use a small circular cutter to create a hoop, and cut through to create a strip. Transfer to a flower mat.

2 With the outside edge of the strip sitting on the edge of the mat, roll the frilling tool back and forth, pressing and stretching the fondant. Rotate the strip. To attach, moisten the reverse with a little water.

For ropes, roll out the fondant on a dusted surface and cut into strips. Roll with your hands to create strands. Moisten the length of one and fix another to each end. Twist each end in the opposite direction.

For chains, cut untwisted ropes into evenly sized pieces. Make a link by moistening the ends of one piece of rope with water, and pressing them together to make a neat join. Repeat, looping each link as you go.

Modelling with marzipan

You can sculpt, smooth, and reshape marzipan as much as you wish, as it is soft and pliable and takes a long time to dry. Marzipan fruits are traditionally used to decorate Christmas fruitcakes. They are pretty, easy to make, and can be created with very little equipment.

Equipment
* veining tool

Ingredients
* cornflour, for dusting
* 200g (7oz) marzipan (see p36)
* 1 tsp tylose powder, optional
* red, brown, and green colouring pastes
* edible glue

Tip
To make edible glue, mix together ¼ teaspoon of finely milled tylose powder with 2 tablespoons of warm water. Mix until most of the lumps have dissolved. Cover and refrigerate overnight. When it is ready, it will have a syrupy consistency.

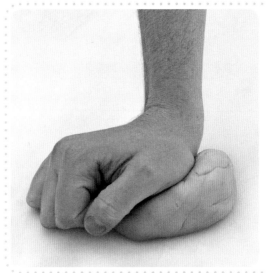

1 Dust a flat surface with cornflour and warm a little marzipan in your hands. Knead it until it is soft and pliable. If you need the decorations to harden more quickly, knead in a little tylose powder (see p87).

2 Break 2 golf ball sized pieces of marzipan from the ball and set aside. Use a cocktail stick to dab red colouring paste into the centre of the rest and knead until evenly distributed. Add more paste until you get the desired colour. Colour one of the golf balls with brown paste and the other with green in the same way.

3 Take a ball of red marzipan and form it into a soft, smooth cone. Press each "strawberry" all over with the end of a cocktail stick, to make seed-like impressions. Poke a hole in the top for the stem.

4 Use the same technique to make the apples, creating slightly rounder cones with a flatter base. Use a veining tool to poke a hole in the centre of each apple.

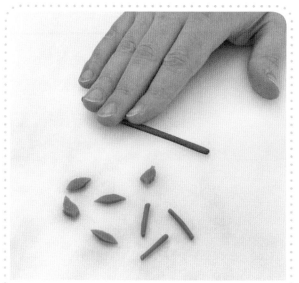

5 Use green marzipan to form leaves and stems. Take a tiny flat, oval piece and then mould until you have the desired shape. Green and brown stems can be made by rolling the marzipan into a narrow rope.

6 Fix the stems into the pieces of fruit using edible glue. Glue one leaf on either side of the brown stem for the apples, and a crown of leaves around the strawberry stems. Allow to harden for about 24 hours.

USING CUTTERS AND MOULDS

An incredible variety of cutters and moulds makes it easy to achieve a professional finish. They are fuss-free and require very little experience. These techniques show you how to use them, providing you with all the specialist guidance you need to create perfect fondant stars, butterflies, and lacework ribbons.

Using plunger cutters

Plunger cutters provide detailed decorative shapes with minimum effort. Use cutters with fondant, flower paste, Mexican paste, and chocolate clay. Try experimenting with layers, shapes, and painted effects to produce a unique array of finished decorations.

Equipment

* fondant roller
* plunger cutters
* forming tray, optional
* flower mat or foam, optional
* ball tool, optional
* dowel or roller, optional

Ingredients

* cornflour, for dusting
* fondant, or any other modelling paste or clay
* tylose powder, to strengthen fondant, (see p87), optional

...detailed decorative shapes with minimum effort

1 Dust a surface with cornflour. Knead the fondant, adding tylose powder for firmer shapes. Roll it out to the desired thickness.

2 Dust the cutters with cornflour. Holding the cutter at the base, press down into the fondant and lift out.

3 With the fondant in the cutter, rub the edges to remove uneven bits. If the cutter does not have embossing, move to step 5.

4 Place the cutter on a surface and press the plunger down firmly. This will emboss designs onto the surface of the shape.

TECHNIQUE CONTINUES • • • •

5 Lift the cutter up so it is just above the surface, and press the plunger again to release your shape. If you are using an embossing cutter, it should now be embossed with the design. These embossed marks are useful when you come to paint or dust decorations.

6 Gently transfer the shapes onto a flower mat or foam. Use a ball tool to shape them and add definition, if desired.

Tip

If the fondant or flower paste sticks to your cutter, dust the cutter with cornflour or lightly grease with white vegetable fat and try again. It can also help to let the fondant dry out for a few minutes before re-cutting your shape.

7 You could release shapes into forming trays to dry in a natural shape for at least 3 hours. Curl shapes around a dowel or roller to give them a natural curve.

Variations

Use cutters to cut out shapes from a sheet of fondant. Where the gaps are left, fill with shapes from another shade of fondant. You can easily remove the plunger and transform the cutter into a basic cookie cutter (see pp106–07).

For more delicate shapes, roll the fondant very thin and allow it to dry for up to 30 minutes, forming a light crust, before cutting. This helps to ensure easy release from the cutter and a clean, even shape. When the shapes are intricate, like this snowflake, run a sharp knife around the edges and into the grooves of the cutter to release any trapped fondant and create a crisp edge.

Plunger cutter designs

Available in an increasing range of shapes and sizes, plunger cutters make cutting simple and embossed shapes easier than ever. They also create quick, accomplished decorations with a perfect finish. Layer, paint, and shape your designs to achieve a unique look.

Butterflies
This cutter embosses with detail. Dry in the crease of an open book to keep the wings upright, or dust with glitter to highlight.

Daisies
Cut out a basic daisy shape with the marguerite daisy cutter. If you avoid pressing down on the plunger when you are cutting, your flowers will be unembossed.

Blossoms
Cut blossoms in a variety of shapes. The ball in the cutter embosses a circular centre that can be topped with a bead of royal icing or fondant, and also curls the petals upwards.

Stars
Star plunger cutters come in many sizes and produce crisp, perfectly formed edges. These simple stars are ideal for cupcake toppers or cakes.

Circles
Circle plunger cutters will become one of the mainstays of your cake-decorating toolkit, and you can use them to cut flawless circles in a variety of sizes.

Hearts
A heart plunger cutter creates uniform shapes that can be painted or sprinkled with glitter for dramatic effect.

Gerbera

Use a marguerite daisy cutter in a variety of sizes to produce a beautiful, layered gerbera. Try poking the centre with a cocktail stick for authentic detail.

Layered stars

Layering multi-coloured shapes in different sizes produces pretty decorations to match your colour theme. Glue them by moistening the backs with water.

Embossed blossoms

Cutting the outline of a blossom rather than embossing the centre gives a good basic shape that can be embossed and dusted.

Embossed hearts

Cut hearts from embossed fondant or flower paste, or run an embossing roller over the surface of the hearts after cutting. Always emboss while the fondant is still soft.

Glitter stars

Cut stars from embossed fondant and sprinkle with glitter or lustre dust to produce a lovely shimmer.

Layered flowers

Simple, unembossed daisies form the basis of these decorations. Allowing them to dry a little before layering helps them to keep their shape.

Using cookie cutters

Use traditional plastic or metal cookie cutters to cut flower paste or fondant into a variety of shapes, such as these hearts and stars. You need to remove the paste from such cutters yourself, while plunger cutters do this for you. Allow the shapes to dry before painting.

Equipment

* ✳ fondant roller
* ✳ cookie cutters
* ✳ flower mat or foam, optional
* ✳ veining, embossing, or ball tools, optional

Ingredients

* ✳ cornflour, for dusting
* ✳ flower paste, other modelling paste, or strengthened fondant (see p87), rolled to the desired thickness
* ✳ edible glue, optional

…create a variety of shapes, such as these hearts and stars

1 Put some cornflour in a plastic bag with the cutters. Shake to coat them, then remove and lightly tap to remove excess flour.

2 Press the cutters into the paste, cutting all the way through. Move the cutter from side to side to release the shapes.

3 Lift the cutter. If the paste sticks to it, use a veining tool to gently push it away from the edges. Moisten with water or edible glue and fix to your cake now, if desired, or move onto baking parchment to dry overnight.

All shapes should be dried and dusted to remove any excess paste or cornflour before painting

Use a palette knife to carefully transfer the decoration to another surface for drying or shaping

5 Use veining or embossing tools to add detail (see p110). Use a ball tool to shape and thin the edges of petals or leaves.

4 If you wish to transfer them to another surface, such as a flower mat, use a palette knife to move them.

6 To use shapes for modelling, such as petals for a rose, loosely cover them in cling film so that they remain pliable.

Mosaic and layering work

Layer different fondant shapes to create textured and multi-coloured decorations. Use small plunger cutters of the same shape to cut tiles, strips, or other shapes, and then join them together for a mosaic effect on a fondant decoration or the surface of a cake.

Equipment

* fondant roller
* cutters
* flower mat or foam, optional
* ball tool, optional

Ingredients

* fondant, or any modelling paste or clay
* cornflour, for dusting
* edible glue, optional

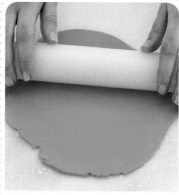

1 For a mosaic tile effect, roll out the fondant to the desired thickness on a surface dusted with cornflour.

2 Cut equally sized squares from the fondant. Moisten with edible glue or water, and paste onto a cake.

Tip

You can cut out pieces from the shapes you have layered on the top, so that the base colour or colours beneath show through. This is a particularly good method for creating windows on houses, buses, or cars.

For inlay patterns, cut out shapes, such as these polka dots, from a flat sheet of fondant. Then cut the same shapes again from a contrasting colour of fondant, and insert these into the first fondant sheet. Gently roll to join and then use to cover your cake or create patterned decorations.

1 **For layered patterns**, such as flowers, place the largest flower shape at the base. Brush the centre with edible glue or water, then place a smaller one on top. Continue with the remaining shapes.

2 You could transfer each shape to a flower mat and use a ball tool to model the petals after you have completed the layering. Leave to set before using edible glue or water to fix to a cake.

For multi-coloured, layered decorations, such as cars, teddies, or faces, cut out various elements of the design in the appropriate colours, using a template if necessary. Moisten the back of each element with a little edible glue or water, and continue layering until all the elements are in place.

Layer daisies
*in bright colours
(see pp104–05).*

Embossing leaves and flowers

Shape and emboss to create realistic leaves and flowers, using one of many embossing and veining mats available. Ball, flower, and leaf tools add shape and definition. Many plunger cutters have veins and other features embedded, so they can do two jobs at once.

Equipment

* veining mat or sheet
* cutting wheel tool, optional
* flower mat or foam
* ball tool
* flower and leaf tool
* cone tool
* flower former, optional

Ingredients

* cornflour, for dusting
* flower paste, modelling paste, or strengthened fondant (see p87)
* white vegetable fat, for greasing

Variation

Use a veiner to create ridges and impressions on fondant and flower-paste leaves. Place the shape on the mat and use the ball tool or your fingers to press it down onto the veiner. Turn it over, and continue with step 3 to enhance the shape.

1 For leaves, press rolled-out flower paste over a cornflour-dusted veining mat, pushing it into all the grooves and ridges.

2 Lift the paste off the mat and turn it over on the dusted surface. Use a cutting wheel tool or a knife to cut the outside edge.

3 Grease the surface of the tools with white vegetable fat, to prevent sticking. Transfer the leaf to the flower mat or foam, using a palette knife, and use the tools to enhance the grooves and ridges. Soften the edges to provide more shape. Leave on the mat to dry and harden overnight, if desired.

1 **For flowers**, dust a surface with cornflour and roll out the paste. Cut out the flowers and leaves and transfer them to a sheet of baking parchment or a flower mat, using a palette knife.

2 To shape the flowers, use the ball tool to press down onto the edges of the petals. Gently move the tool towards the centre of the flower to encourage the petals to form into cups.

3 Use the flower and leaf tool to score veins into the petals, to give them a realistic, textured appearance. To hollow out the centre of the flower, press the cone tool into the middle of the shape. This is a good way to make holes through which wire and stamens can later be added. Leave on the mat to dry overnight, or transfer the blossoms to a flower former, if desired, so that they dry in a curved shape.

Creating flower sprays

All you need to create realistic sprays – displays of cascading flowers and leaves – are a few simple tools. Sprays can be informal tumbles or traditional bouquets, depending on the celebration. Wire them individually and then group them together on top of a cake.

Equipment

* 22- or 24-gauge florist's wire
* wire cutters
* needle-nose pliers
* florist's tape
* flower and leaf tool
* florist oasis or Styrofoam, to keep flowers upright
* veining mat or mould
* ball tool, optional

Ingredients

* flower-paste or fondant flowers and leaves
* flower paste or strengthened fondant (see p87)
* edible glue

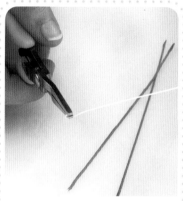

1 Cut a length of florist's wire, then bend the tip into a loop with needle-nose pliers. Wrap the loop with florist's tape.

2 Form the paste into a small cone and press the loop into the centre. Press down to get a flat end. Dab with edible glue.

3 Press the flower onto the flat surface. Hold for a minute to allow it to adhere. Place in an oasis or a piece of Styrofoam.

4 Use a cutter or veining mat to cut out leaves thick enough for a wire to be inserted. Thin the edges with a ball tool.

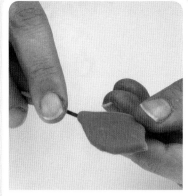

5 A veining mat creates a useful ridge in the centre of leaves. Slip wire into the ridge and tape it while the paste is soft.

Variations

Wire hand-modelled flowers, such as roses, as you make them (see p88). Flowers with holes in the centre help with wiring – moisten the loop wire and press it onto the flower centre. Moisten the centre with edible glue or water and then feed the wire through.

6 Once dry, wrap together the wires of a leaf or two with florist's tape, then attach to the base of one of the flowers.

Pull the florist's tape up around the joins of the wire and press firmly to adhere

Wrap each flower stem individually

One by one, add more flowers and leaves to the flower spray

Embossing a patchwork design

You can use patchwork cutters to beautifully emboss the surface of a fondant-covered cake, or to create an interesting plaque. Emboss other decorative pieces that can then be painted, piped, or used as the basis for layered decorations on a cake or structure.

Equipment

* ✳ fondant roller
* ✳ patchwork cutters
* ✳ lustre dust or spray, optional
* ✳ edible paint or felt-tip pen, optional

Ingredients

* ✳ white vegetable fat, for greasing
* ✳ fondant-covered cake or sheet of rolled fondant

Emboss decorative pieces that can be painted, piped, or used for layered decorations

To emboss a cake surface, lightly grease the patchwork cutters with white vegetable fat and emboss all or part of a fondant-covered cake. Press the cutters firmly into the surface of the fondant. You can highlight or paint the impressions with lustre dust or spray (see p136).

To emboss a plaque, or any other decoration using rolled-out fondant, cut it to the desired shape, then press the cutter into the surface. Place it on baking parchment to dry. You can pipe the design or use edible paint or felt-tip pens to highlight the impressions (see p137).

Cutting a patchwork design

Try patchwork cutters to cut out a variety of shapes from flower paste, Mexican paste, or fondant, ready to fix onto your cake. Very thin decorations are easier to cut, but will dry out more quickly. Push the cutter into the paste with a firm pressure and lift it out gently.

Equipment

* fondant roller
* patchwork cutter

Ingredients

* white vegetable fat, for greasing
* flower paste, other modelling paste, or strengthened fondant (see p87)
* edible glue

1 Lightly grease a flat surface and the patchwork cutter with white vegetable fat. Roll out the paste to the desired thickness.

2 Press the entire outline of the cutter firmly to cut through the paste and then lightly press the central sections to emboss it.

3 Remove any excess paste, with the cutter in place. Use a palette knife to lift the shape onto baking parchment to dry.

4 Affix decorations to the surface of a cake, or leave to dry overnight and place upright on it, brushing with edible glue.

Tip
An easy way to release the design from the patchwork cutter is to gently press the paste with your finger from the back of the cutter. You could also use a veiner or the end of a cocktail stick to gently detach the paste from the intricate edges.

Making a patchwork design

Build up a patchwork design to add detail and create an almost 3D effect. You can build the design directly on your cake or on a piece of baking parchment, allowing it to dry and placing it flat or upright on the finished cake. Always start with the largest section of the design.

Equipment
* patchwork cutters
* fondant roller

Ingredients
* white vegetable fat, for greasing
* flower paste, modelling paste, or strengthened fondant (see p87)
* edible glue

...add detail and create an almost 3D effect

1 Apply a patchwork cutter, greased with white vegetable fat, directly into a flower-paste plaque to leave an impression.

2 Store the pastes in plastic bags to keep them pliable. Choose colours for each section, then roll them out thinly.

3 Cut out the largest piece of the design. Position it on the embossed design and trim or press into shape as necessary.

4 Working with 1 colour at a time, cut and fix the pieces into place over the main design with edible glue, until complete.

Using tappits

Tappits are similar to patchwork cutters, but they come in strips that are pressed down into lengths of rolled fondant or paste, pressed through to cut, and then tapped out. Use them for creating delicate decorations or even neat numbers, letters, and other small shapes.

Equipment

* fondant roller
* tappit set, with rectangle cutter
* foam, optional

Ingredients

* white vegetable fat, for greasing
* sheet of strengthened fondant (see p87), or modelling paste
* edible dust, optional
* edible glue

Tip

To release the cut designs from the tappits, tap them firmly against the corner of a hard surface before laying them on foam or baking parchment to dry. If they have lost their shape, adjust gently with your fingers or a veining tool.

1 Lightly grease the fondant and tappits. Place the strip cutter on the fondant and press down to cut. Remove excess fondant.

2 Place the tappit across the strip horizontally to cut one shape at a time. Press firmly so the edges cut right through.

3 Use a sharp knife to remove excess fondant. Use a palette knife to lift onto baking parchment or foam to dry until firm.

4 If desired, you can dust or paint the designs with edible dust before sticking them to your cake with edible glue.

Using multi-ribbon cutters

You can roll multi-ribbon cutters over the top of a sheet of paste or fondant to cut and emboss ribbons of all shapes and sizes. Decorate your cakes with ribbons or use strengthened fondant (see p87) or paste ribbons to to create a variety of different stripes, bows, and swags.

Equipment
* fondant roller
* multi-ribbon cutter set

Ingredients
* sheet of fondant, flower paste, or other modelling paste
* cornflour, for dusting

...different stripes, bows, and swags to decorate cakes

Tips
Change the look of the ribbons by ruffling the edges (see p97). Allow to set for a moment or two before applying to your cake, so they hold their shape, but don't wait too long or the fondant may crack.

1 Assemble the roller, using spacers to make the ribbons the desired width, and the cutting wheels to produce the impression you want. Use wavy, beaded, or zigzag cutters for a variety of styles. Add spacers and tighten the bolt so that the wheels move backwards and forwards, instead of from side to side.

2 Place the fondant on a surface dusted with cornflour. Press the ribbon cutter into the fondant at the edge closest to you, and press down on the roller, so that it cuts through the fondant to the surface beneath. Continuing to press hard, roll the cutter away from you firmly but gently. Repeat and trim excess with a sharp knife.

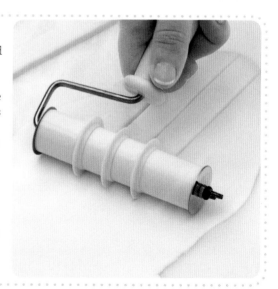

Using flat ribbon cutters

Flat ribbon cutters work like patchwork cutters or tappits, cutting the outside edges while embossing the surface. They can produce embossed, flat, frilled, ribbed, or scalloped ribbons. There are two ways to use these types of cutters, both of which result in flawless ribbons.

Equipment
* flat ribbon cutter
* fondant roller

Ingredients
* sheet of fondant, flower paste, or other modelling paste, cut into ribbon-width lengths
* cornflour, for dusting

Create frilled, ribbed, or scalloped ribbons

Variations
Apply ribbons to your cake by moistening their reverse with water or a little edible glue. You could wrap them around supports and dry them overnight, to create twists, bows, and other shapes. Apply these designs to your cake once they are dry.

To lay the fondant on the cutter, place the cutter flat on a cornflour-dusted surface, with the cutting edges facing upwards. Gently lift the fondant on top, to cover the surface, and use the roller to press the fondant into the cutting edges. Remove any excess, turn over the cutter, and tap to release the ribbons.

To lay the cutter on the fondant, place the cutter into the fondant, and use the fondant roller to press it firmly into the surface, working from one end of the cutter to the other. Gently pull the cutter away from the paste to release the ribbons.

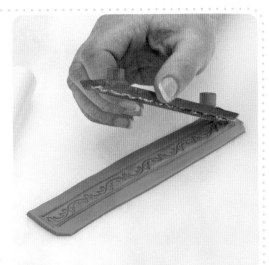

Using silicone moulds

Use these pliable moulds to create everything from attractive cupcake and miniature cake toppers to decorative elements for a whole cake. It is crucial to grease or dust moulds well, so that you can remove the fondant shapes in one piece and with minimal effort.

Equipment
* clean silicone mould

Ingredients
* white vegetable fat, for greasing
* cornflour, for dusting
* fondant (strengthened, if desired; see p87), flower paste, or modelling paste

1 Grease a silicone mould with white vegetable fat or dust it with cornflour. Make sure the fat or flour enters all the crevices.

2 Knead the fondant into a soft, pliable ball. Press the ball into the mould, using your thumb so that it fills the mould completely.

Variation
You can use different colours of fondant in a single mould, pressing small amounts of each colour into the detail. Use a single base colour to fill the mould to the top and join all the pieces together. Continue with steps 3 and 4.

3 Cut off any excess and dry for a few minutes. If the fondant is not strengthened, place it in the freezer for a few minutes.

4 Bend the mould so the shape falls out. Trim the edges and moisten the back with water to apply to the cake, or allow to dry.

Using plastic moulds

Plastic moulds, like those used for chocolate moulding (see p60), are ideal for producing 3D designs and decorations. If you are using a deep or wide mould, remember to allow plenty of time for the fondant shape to dry so that it holds its shape.

Equipment

* large plastic mould

Ingredients

* cornflour, for dusting
* flower paste, or other modelling paste, or strengthened fondant (see p87)

...ideal for producing 3D designs and decorations

Tip
To paint the shape, wait until it is just dry to the touch – it needn't be completely dry, so test it after about an hour. Use a clean, dry brush to dust away excess flour, and blot with a kitchen towel to remove fat before you begin painting.

1 Brush the mould well with cornflour and remove any excess. Knead the flower paste into a soft, pliable ball.

2 Press the ball into the mould, applying firm pressure with your thumb to ensure that all the details are filled.

3 Trim any excess from around the mould with a sharp knife. Freeze for up to 30 minutes, or until the paste is firm.

4 Tap the mould, then twist the opposite corners slightly so the shape falls out, flat side down. Dry on baking parchment.

Using resin moulds

Resin moulds often come with a piece of silicone in their centre, which you can use to press paste deep into the mould and also to cut the edges. Resin moulds are particularly useful for creating lacework (as below), scallops, borders, beading, and decorative embellishments.

Equipment

* resin mould with silicone insert
* fondant roller
* ball tool
* wire brush
* straight pin

Ingredients

* cornflour, for dusting
* Mexican paste, strengthened fondant (see p87), or other modelling paste
* edible dust, optional
* edible glue, optional

Variations

Use hard resin moulds to create details, such as facial features and even heads. Resin allows your design to hold its shape better, and minimizes distortion, making it ideal for lacework. Use white vegetable fat instead of cornflour, if desired.

1 Dust the inside of the mould with cornflour, and then tap on a hard surface to remove any excess. Roll out the Mexican paste as thin as you can, on a hard surface dusted with cornflour.

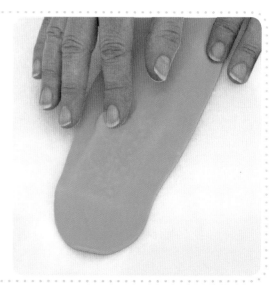

2 Carefully lift the rolled paste over the mould and use your fingers to press it into the grooves.

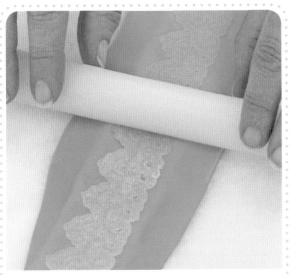

3 Lay the silicone insert on top of the paste and use the roller to push it downwards, embossing the paste. Cut away the excess paste from the edges of the mould with a sharp knife.

4 Remove the silicone insert and rub the end of the ball tool over the raised areas to release any paste where there will be embossed details or cutaways.

5 Use a wire brush over the whole surface of the paste to remove any loose pieces. Use a straight pin to carefully lift up one end of the paste in the mould, and then pull upwards and out of the mould.

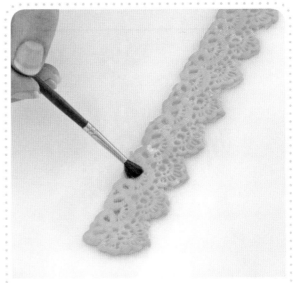

6 Brush with edible dust, if desired, and attach to the cake with edible glue or a little water, if desired. Alternatively, you could dry the lace over a support for use with 3D decorations.

STENCILLING

Stencilling produces a magnificent series of textures, designs, and finishes on any icing surface, with professional-looking and pristine results. You can use shop-bought stencils in myriad ways — such as simple painted or dusted designs, royal-iced intricate damask-style patterns, and embossed features.

Stencilling the sides of a cake

Create beautiful designs to surround cakes or mini cakes using royal icing and a stencil. This is a technique that can take a little practice to get right, so do a few trial runs on a length of fondant before attempting to stencil directly onto your finished cake.

Equipment

* stencil
* masking tape
* fondant smoother

Ingredients

* icing sugar, for dusting
* royal-iced or fondant-covered cake
* royal icing, for piping (see p35)
* colouring paste, if desired

Tips

For a smoother finish, and ease of movement, use a flat-edged icing scraper or stoneware scraper instead of a palette knife to apply the royal icing. If you smudge any of the design, use a cocktail stick to scrape it away.

1 Dust the back of the stencil with a little icing sugar. Place the stencil directly on the surface of the cake, in the position you would like the design to appear. Use masking tape to secure the stencil into place on the cake. Use a fondant smoother to press firmly down on the stencil, in order to lightly emboss.

2 Colour your royal icing, if desired. Spread it thinly over the stencil using a palette knife, moving in one direction only. Allow to dry and then move the stencil, wipe it clean, and repeat as desired around the cake. Allow each design to set fully before moving the stencil, so that you do not smudge the pattern.

Stencilling with royal icing

This is a quick way to create detailed decorations for cakes. Make sure you use piping-consistency royal icing, or the icing may run under the edges of the stencil cut-outs and smear the design. The icing should be roughly the consistency of toothpaste (see p35).

Equipment
* stencil
* masking tape
* fondant roller

Ingredients
* icing sugar, for dusting
* fondant or royal-icing covered square cake
* royal icing, for piping (see p35)

A quick way to create detailed designs

1 Dust the back of the stencil with a little icing sugar, to prevent it from sticking to the surface of the cake. Place the stencil directly onto the surface of the cake, in the position you would like the design to appear. Use masking tape to hold the stencil in place.

2 Press the stencil down into the fondant and run the fondant roller over the top, so that the pattern is lightly embossed, with the fondant just rising above the surface of the stencil.

Tip
When the royal icing begins to form a crust on top of your stencil (step 3), you could apply edible dust to add colour and texture. Rub a little white vegetable fat over the surface of the stencil, and use a large, soft brush to apply the dust.

3 Using a palette knife, spread the royal icing thinly over the surface of the stencil, using gentle strokes in 1 direction. Cover the whole stencil in icing, to be sure you have not missed any parts of the design.

4 Leave the stencil in place for about 10 minutes, so that the icing begins to set. Carefully lift off the stencil, pulling upwards from one corner and peeling it across, to reveal the design beneath. Tidy up your design with a cocktail stick.

Stencilling with paint

It is easier to stencil with paint than it is with royal icing, and you can achieve a variety of dramatic effects. Make sure the fondant or buttercream has set for at least 24 hours, so that the surface has developed a crust before you begin. The paint needs to be thick to avoid running.

Equipment
* stencil

Ingredients
* white vegetable fat, for greasing
* fondant-covered or buttercream-iced cake
* petal or lustre dust mixed with rejuvenator spirit or vodka

...you can achieve a variety of dramatic effects

Variations
Avoid water-based food-colouring paints or gels, as these can run. For quick and easy coverage, try airbrushing the stencil (see pp144–45). Use thin coats and build up a final colour. You could even use undiluted airbrush paints with a brush.

1 Grease the back of the stencil with a little white vegetable fat and press it onto the cake in the desired position.

2 Dip a small paintbrush into a little paint. Paint around the edges of the pattern, onto the surface of the cake.

3 Next, paint inside the edges you have painted, using small, fine strokes to apply even coverage over the whole pattern.

4 Allow the paint to dry completely, before removing the stencil. Fix mistakes with a cotton bud dipped in rejuvenator spirit.

Stencilling with edible dust

You can use any dry edible dusts with a stencil, to create subtle patterns on the top and sides of your cake. Dust over the stencil or stipple with a wide brush, but make sure that you do not tip any onto the cake when lifting off the stencil.

Equipment
* stencil
* masking tape, optional

Ingredients
* white vegetable fat, for greasing
* fondant-covered or buttercream-iced cake
* pearl, lustre, or petal dust

Create subtle patterns on the top and sides of a cake

Tip
If you are using a single stencil wrapped around the circumference of a fondant-covered cake, grease the back of the stencil with a little white vegetable fat so it will stick to the surface. Otherwise, use masking tape to secure it into place.

1 Grease the back of the stencil with a little white vegetable fat and press it onto the cake in the desired position. You could use a little masking tape to create "handles" on either side of the stencil. Place a little dust in a small sieve and gently shake it across the surface of the stencil.

2 Lift off the stencil, taking care to ensure that it remains flat so that none of the dust on the stencil drops onto the cake.

Stencil embossing

Use this technique with any stencil that will lie flat on a surface. You could emboss a sheet of fondant before using it to cover a cake, for a completely decorated surface, or simply emboss decorations, such as a border, for a textured finish. Enhance your designs with lustre dust.

Equipment

* stencil
* fondant roller
* veining tool, optional

Ingredients

* white vegetable fat, for greasing
* sheet of fondant, strengthened if desired (see p87), or rolled buttercream (see p27)
* edible dust

Variations

Use edible felt-tip pens to paint the surface of embossed fondant, for subtle shading, or fully coloured designs. Pens are easier to control than paintbrushes, particularly for intricate designs. Let each section dry before moving on to the next.

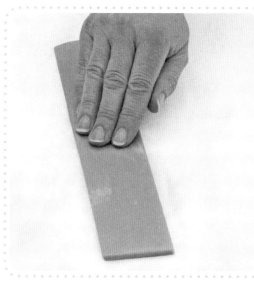

1 Lightly grease the surface of the fondant with a little white vegetable fat. This prevents the stencil from slipping and sticking to the surface of the fondant when it has been embossed, and also helps to fix any dusts you may wish to use after embossing.

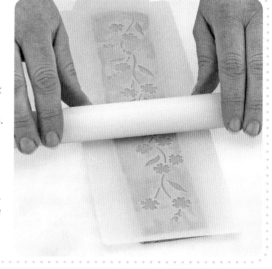

2 Place the stencil on the surface of the fondant and, using the roller, roll it firmly across the stencil, pressing it down so that fondant begins to poke out of the cut-out edges. If you are using a large stencil on a length of rolled-out fondant, work from the inside of the stencil outwards, until the entire surface is evenly embossed.

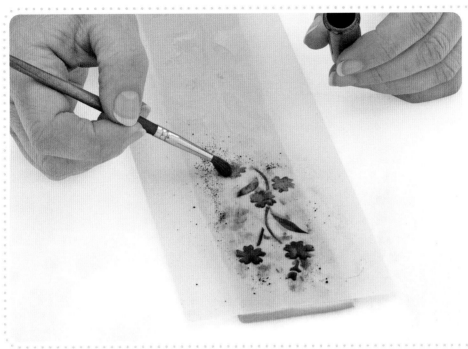

3 With a small paintbrush dust the surface of the stencil with edible dust, using light strokes or stipples to ensure that the entire pattern is covered. Leave for 1–2 hours to allow the dust to set, and then use a soft brush to remove any excess.

4 Remove the stencil and use the end of a sharp knife, or a cotton bud, to clear away any areas where the dust has escaped the outlines of the design. If the pattern is unevenly embossed, or you wish to add more detail, use a veining tool to carefully press down the fondant around the design.

Stencil designs

Paint, dust, royal ice, airbrush, or spray stencils to create wonderful designs on cakes and decorations. You can also use them to emboss any medium, for a highly textured effect. Get the most from each stencil by repeating patterns, or picking out particular details you like.

Butterfly

A diluted colour wash gives this butterfly an ethereal look, which would work well on floral-themed cakes or cupcakes.

Damask

Paint or royal ice a line of these stencils around a wedding cake, or use, one by one, for the sides or tops of cakes and mini cakes, or as a fondant cupcake topper.

Crewel embroidery

Spread this stencil with white or tinted royal icing or carefully paint it with diluted dust. It can be beautiful on the sides or top of a cake.

Butterfly

Use lustre spray to achieve an even coverage of the stencilled area. Repeat the pattern in different colours on cupcakes or around a cake.

Butterfly

Use a fine-tipped point brush to achieve delicate outlines for this pretty butterfly and dot amongst stencilled flowers and foliage.

Skull and crossbones

A colour wash makes this image suitably weather-worn. Try on pirate cupcakes or the rice paper sails of a ship.

Imperial crown

Dilute lustre dust with rejuvenator spirit, stencil onto strengthened fondant, then cut around, dry, and use as a decoration.

Coronation crown

Brush with pale gold lustre dust for a softer appearance or use to emboss the surface of cupcakes and mini cakes for royal celebrations.

Violet wallpaper

Repeat this crewel embroidery pattern across the surface of a cake, brushing with lilac paint to create an elegant, antique wallpaper design.

Decorative roses

Sponge pink and green petal dusts, thinned with rejuvenator spirit, to create a delicate spray of roses on a cake or cupcake top, or a simple plaque.

Russet sprigs

Select detail from a larger stencil and sponge or stipple with light and darker shades of the same colour for a burnished appearance.

Tumbling teddies

Paint the teddies with soft aqua around the base of a fondant-covered cake or on a thin strip of flower paste. Individual teddies make pretty toppers for cupcakes or mini cakes.

PAINTING

Achieve a spectacular finish and intricate, textured designs with painting or airbrushing. Paint your cakes and decorations with a range of edible dusts, tints, pastes, paints, and pens. Create smooth, flawless royal-icing runouts, or dappled, dotted fondant surfaces. Use a variety of different textures and special effects to make your creations unique.

Using edible liquid paints

Apply these ready-to-use edible paints to decorations with a brush or sponge (see p147). Use a broad brush for easier application on large surfaces. It is best to cover as much of the decoration as you can with each stroke, as multiple layers can make the surface uneven.

Ingredients

* fondant ribbons
* edible liquid paint
* rejuvenator spirit or vodka

...cover as much of the decoration as you can with each stroke

Tips

Always clean the brushes with rejuvenator spirit or vodka as many paints harden in water, making the brush unusable. If the paint dries out while you are working, or it becomes too thick, stir in a little rejuvenator spirit to thin it out.

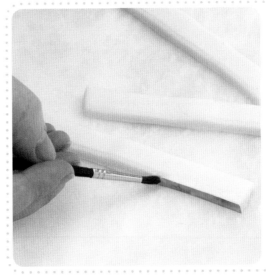

1 Lay the ribbons on a flat surface, leaving a gap between each. Brush them with a soft brush to remove excess cornflour. Shake the paint well, before pouring a small amount onto a plate or paint palette. Dip a paintbrush in the paint and carefully apply to the sides of the ribbons using straight, even strokes.

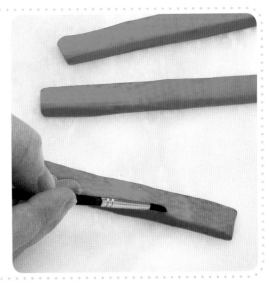

2 Paint the top of the ribbons in the same way, ideally in just a few long strokes. If the finish is uneven, allow the paint to dry completely before adding a second coat. You can use these versatile ribbons in so many ways – from bright stripes for a train cake, to wooden planks on a pirate ship cake.

Using edible dusts

You can paint entire cakes with edible dusts, or simply add shimmer and colour to small decorations. Paint made from edible dust dries very quickly, so use a little and work as fast as you can – it is better to use several coats of thin paint than to use one layer of thick paint.

Ingredients

* edible dust
* rejuvenator spirit or vodka
* dry fondant or flower-paste decorations

...simply add shimmer and colour

Variations

Mix dusts and powders to create new shades, or add lustre dust for shimmer. To paint large areas with blended colours, mix up a large quantity, but add spirit a little at a time. If the spirit evaporates, add more to the powder if needed, or store away.

1 Place a small amount of dust in a ramekin and add a few drops of rejuvenator spirit. Mix until smooth to create a "paint".

2 For overall colour, apply the paint from the inside outwards, to avoid a pool of paint in the centre. Allow to dry.

3 Refresh the ramekin with spirit. When the first coat is dry, paint another. Use a thin brush for detailing, if desired.

4 For a gentle tint or lustre, allow the paint to dry and brush on dry dust rather than using the spirit to create a paint.

Using edible felt-tip pens

Use edible felt-tip pens to paint fine details and write directly onto fondant-covered cakes and fondant or flower-paste decorations. Use the pens with stencils or on embossed surfaces to provide colour and detail, or try them freehand. They are widely available in broad or fine tips.

Ingredients

* dry fondant or flower-paste decorations
* edible felt-tip pens
* rejuvenator spirit or vodka, optional

...paint fine details and write directly onto fondant

Variations

Emboss a design onto a cake using a cutter or a template. Choose broad edible felt-tip pens to colour, using even strokes on small areas, and fine-tipped pens for crisp outlines. Dip a paintbrush in rejuvenator spirit to smudge or thin the inked surfaces.

1 Place the decorations on a flat, firm surface, and support any parts that might shift or wobble while you work. Fill in larger areas first, using a broad or fine pen, depending on the size of the area that needs coverage.

2 Use a finer pen to create outlines and finer details, highlight your work, provide contrast, or cover any messy edges. Store the pens upside down. If the pens form crystals, dip them in rejuvenator spirit for a minute or two, put on the caps and shake. Let them rest for 15 minutes before using.

Using colouring pastes

Use colouring pastes for painting, as well as for adding colour to icings, modelling clays and pastes, and fondant. You can use more rejuvenator spirit to create a thinner paint for colour washes, stippling, or sponging, or less to create denser blocks of colour with a paintbrush.

Ingredients

* colouring pastes
* rejuvenator spirit or vodka
* fondant-covered cake, or fondant or flower-paste decoration

Vary shades to create contrasting effects

Tip

Colouring paste can be thinned with water, but it tends to give a less even coverage and have an increased drying time, so instead mix with rejuvenator spirit or vodka – great when you are under time pressure as it dries so much more quickly.

1 Use a cocktail stick to place a little colouring paste in a ramekin. Add a few drops of rejuvenator spirit to the paste, and stir with the cocktail stick until absorbed and the paint is loose and smooth.

2 Apply the paint immediately with a paintbrush, adding a little more rejuvenator spirit to keep it fluid.

Brushwork embroidery

Use royal icing to create beautiful, textured designs on a variety of cakes or decorations, with just a cutter and a paintbrush. This technique is called brushwork embroidery because the finished result is very much like a detailed, embroidered surface.

Equipment

✳ cutter, to emboss
✳ piping bag with a narrow round piping tip

Ingredients

✳ fondant-covered or smooth-iced cakes
✳ royal icing (coloured, if desired, see pp34–35), thinned out with a little water

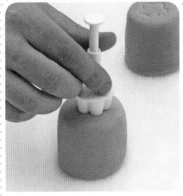

1 Lightly emboss an outline on the cake surface using a cutter. Allow the fondant to set for a few hours.

2 Fill the piping bag with royal icing. Working on one part of the design at a time, pipe over the embossed outline.

Tips

Keep the brush damp. You will be able to make 3 or 4 strokes before it needs to be dipped into water again. After the brushwork, pipe details, such as centres for flowers or stems for leaves, if desired. Allow to dry.

3 Dip a paintbrush in water, and draw it through the icing towards the centre of the design, using small, even strokes.

4 Continue to pull the icing into the centre of the design, until the shape is complete. Pipe more detail onto the design.

Piping royal icing runouts

Royal icing runout, also known as "flood work", involves piping royal icing into a shape and allowing it to dry until hard. You can use the decoration as part of a 3D cake topping, or lay it flat to embellish cakes, cookies, gingerbread, and cupcakes. Be careful, as it will be fragile.

Equipment

* food-grade acetate sheets
* cardboard or baking parchment template
* 2 piping bags, 1 fitted with a small, fine round tip and the other with a large round tip

Ingredients

* white vegetable fat, for greasing
* royal icing (see pp34–35), tinted or coloured as desired

Variations

For thick, sturdy runouts, apply several coats of piped icing. Allow each coat to dry for 24 hours. Produce multi-coloured runouts by filling areas with royal icing in different colours. So long as there is no break in the outline, the icing will hold its shape.

1 Lay the acetate sheet directly onto the template so that the template is visible through the surface. Lightly grease the acetate with white vegetable fat. You could also lay the template on top of a piece of baking parchment and trace the shape, if preferred.

2 Using the small, fine tip, pipe royal icing around the outline of the shape. Allow this to dry for a couple of hours to create a "dam", or if you are using different colours on the surface of your decoration, pipe in outlines now, and then leave everything to dry.

3 The royal icing needs to be thinned for the runout stage. Spritz the royal icing with water, or add it drop by drop until the icing is roughly the consistency of shampoo. Draw a spoon through the surface. If the line created fills in 10 seconds, it is the right consistency for flooding. Fill a piping bag attached to the large tip, with the thin royal icing. Press down on the piping bag and "flood" the template with icing, working from the centre outwards until the entire surface of the design is covered. When the flooding is complete, gently tap the board to release any air bubbles that will make the shape more fragile.

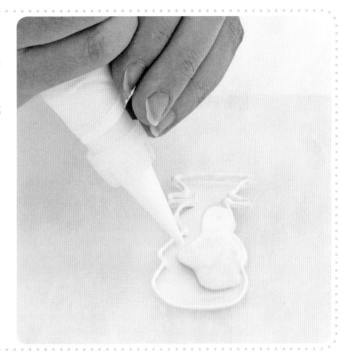

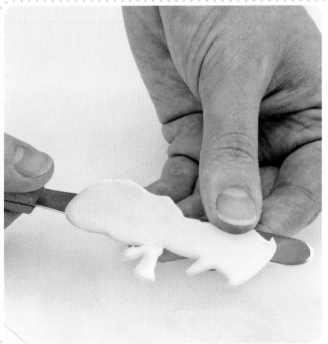

4 Allow to dry for 24 hours before applying details, such as additional piping or painting. Lift the decoration away from the acetate sheet with a palette knife and carefully apply to the cake with a dab of royal icing. Alternatively, you could attach to a cake-pop stick or wire with a dab of royal icing.

Runout designs *are easily layered (see pp220–22).*

Painting flowers

Tinting or painting flowers makes them look realistic, even if you have used coloured fondant or modelling paste. You can dust flowers and leaves moulded from flower paste in the same way – and you can go one step further by steaming them lightly to add sheen.

Equipment

* Styrofoam or florist oasis, optional

Ingredients

* flower-paste roses, or other fondant or modelling paste flowers
* lustre or blossom tint dusts
* rejuvenator spirit or vodka, optional

Steam flower-paste decorations lightly to add sheen

Tips

Do not steam the flower for longer than a few seconds or it may disintegrate. As soon as it takes on a light sheen, remove it from the steam and place it on baking parchment or Styrofoam to dry. Try holding the wire with tongs.

1 Lay the flowers on a flat surface. They will need to be completely dry. If the flowers are wired, place them in Styrofoam so that they stand upright.

2 Place some lustre dust on a plate and dip a paintbrush into it. Apply carefully to the inside of the petals, and work outwards, pulling the brush along the surface of the petals to the edge. Use slightly darker tints of the same colour at the centre of the petals and along the top edges to provide realistic contrast and definition.

3 Apply the dust to the outside of the flower in small, even strokes, working from the bottom to the top. If desired, mix together a little dust with some rejuvenator spirit (see p136) to create a smooth paint, and apply this where you want the colours to be darkest – at the base of the petals, for example. If your flowers are made from fondant or modelling paste, don't steam them (see below). Instead, allow to dry overnight before applying to your cake.

To steam flower-paste flowers, fill a small pan with water and bring to the boil. Hold each flower over the steam for a few seconds, until the paste takes on a wet appearance. This sets the dust and the colour. Turn the flower to ensure all surfaces come into contact with the steam.

Flower-paste orchids *can also be tinted (see pp90–91).*

Airbrushing

Use an airbrushing machine to create an even base colour for iced cakes, or to add detail and shading to cakes, stencil designs, and decorations. Although airbrushing can take time to master (practise on kitchen paper or newspaper), the results are well worth the effort.

Equipment

* airbrushing machine

Ingredients

* fondant-covered cake
* edible liquid paints
* rejuvenator spirit or vodka, optional

...create an even base colour for iced cakes

Variation

Use airbrushing to give definition to 3D cakes and decorations; for example, spray a darker orange into the grooves of a pumpkin, add a lighter shade to the centre surface of a balloon, use for a detailed stencil, or give detail to a handbag cake.

1 Cover the area around the cake, including the board, with newspaper or baking parchment. Load the airbrushing machine with the edible liquid paint. Holding the nozzle about 20cm (8in) from the cake and at a 45° angle, spray over the top using long, sweeping movements.

2 Allow the layer to dry. Remove the paint and clean out the pipes of the machine to ensure that the colours do not run and the needle is clear enough to provide a uniform, even spray. Load the next colour into the machine.

3 Holding the nozzle at a 90° angle will create a more defined line, which is perfect for this rainbow design. Starting at the base, spray the first colour, changing the angle of the nozzle to produce the desired effect.

4 Clean the machine again, and load the next colour, spraying this next to the first colour as evenly as possible. It is better to layer light swathes of colour rather than spraying too much in one go.

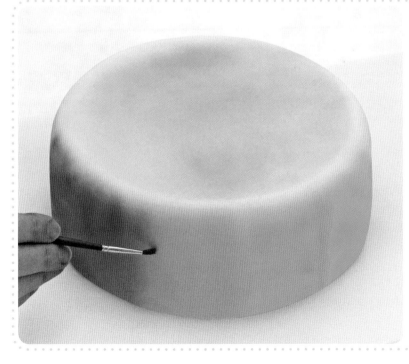

5 Continue until all the colours are in place. You could neaten the edges of the design with the blade of a sharp knife, or blur the edges a little with a paintbrush dipped in rejuvenator spirit (as shown here).

Tips

You can make colours darker by retracing over them with the airbrushing machine. Unless you wish to create a secondary colour, try to avoid spraying one colour on top of another, as they will blend (creating new colour shades).

Painting a colour wash

Colour washes can highlight embossing, pick out textures on decorations, and provide a light background for further design work. You will need very diluted ready-made paint, or you can mix your own from colouring dust or paste and rejuvenator spirit (see p136 and p138).

Ingredients

* edible liquid paint, colouring paste, or dusts in 2 colours
* rejuvenator spirit or vodka
* embossed fondant-covered cake

...provide a light background for further design work

Variations

"Drag" by painting the surface with 1 colour, and gently brushing the cake in one direction and then the other using a clean, dry paintbrush. "Rag-roll" by using a balled-up piece of kitchen paper to apply and remove paint and create a mottled effect.

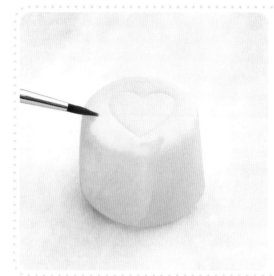

1 Dilute the paint with rejuvenator spirit to create a wash. Using a paintbrush, wash the paint over the embossed cake. You can cover evenly or unevenly, depending on the look you want. For a darker shade, colour wash the cake a second time and allow the excess paint to pool in the embossed grooves.

2 Paint some of the smaller areas or detailed sections of your embossed design, such as this heart, with another colour wash. You may wish to use a smaller brush for finer details like this. Allow to dry.

Stippling and sponging

These methods help you to create different textures on the surface of cakes or decorations. Use a stippling brush or specialized sponge to produce a subtle finish with tiny dots of colour. Sponging achieves a dappled result; try playing around with layers in different shades.

Equipment
* stippling brush or sponge
* sponge

Ingredients
* edible liquid paint, colouring paste, or dusts
* rejuvenator spirit or vodka
* fondant-covered or smooth-iced cakes

...create different textures on the surface of cakes

Tips
Stipple, wash, or sponge shades of the same colour in layers to produce a textured look. Try sponging a lighter shade of a colour over a darker base, for the look of fabric. Dab the sponge heavily over some parts to look like velvet.

1 **To stipple**, lightly dip the stippling brush into edible liquid paint, heavily diluted with rejuvenator spirit.

2 Dot your brush on the surface of the cake in an up-and-down motion. Allow to dry and repeat, if desired.

1 **To sponge**, you could use thicker paint for a bolder result. Dip the sponge into the paint and apply to the cake.

2 Rinse your sponge. Apply a second colour for a textured look. To avoid muddying, allow to dry before applying new colours.

IMAGING

*Digital imaging – on edible icing sheets or
rice paper – has transformed the cake-decorating world.
Make your creations personal and add accurate details
using images or patterns. Print at home on an adapted
printer or commission from a specialist supplier, to
create prints that you can easily fix to your cakes.*

Using rice paper

Rice paper is available in different colours, patterns, and pretty prints. It can be folded and bent without cracking, which makes it perfect for these butterfly designs. Decorate with edible glitter, if you wish, and attach them to cakes with royal icing or edible glue.

Ingredients

* sheet of rice paper, printed with edible ink
* piping gel, optional
* edible glitter, optional

You can fold or bend rice paper designs without cracking them

1 Lay out your rice paper sheet on a flat surface and carefully cut out the images. Transfer them to some baking parchment until you wish to use them for decorating. For a sparkly touch, prepare the shapes by painting them with piping gel and leaving them to dry for a few hours, ideally overnight.

Variation

If you are printing on rice paper yourself – using a printer set up with edible ink – make sure the rice paper is sturdy enough to absorb the ink without dissolving. Check with the supplier to ensure that the paper is appropriate for printing.

2 When the gel is gummy, sprinkle over the edible glitter. You could fold the paper gently, if appropriate, for a 3D effect – perfect here for the wings of a butterfly. Leave them to dry in the crease of an open hardback book so they dry in shape, before attaching to your cake with royal icing or edible glue.

Using icing sheets

Send an image to a specialist company and they can print it for you on icing sheets. To use, cut out and apply directly to the top of your cakes – or stick them onto rolled flower paste or strengthened fondant first. The sheets must be kept in an zip-locked bag or they will dry out.

Equipment

* fondant roller

Ingredients

* printed icing sheet
* cornflour, for dusting
* strengthened fondant (see p87)
* cupcakes piped with buttercream icing, optional

...apply images to rolled, strengthened fondant

Tips

You can wrap icing sheets with ready-printed patterns on them around the sides of your cake. Why not try leopard print for a handbag cake, or fairies and butterflies for a little girl's cake? The possiblities are endless.

1 Carefully cut out all the images from the icing sheet with scissors and set aside. Dust a surface with cornflour and roll out the fondant to the desired thickness.

2 Moisten the surface of the fondant with a little water, using a pastry brush, and then arrange the images on top, as closely together as possible. Allow to dry for a few minutes and then cut out the images on the fondant, using a sharp knife.

3 Place the images on a piece of baking parchment, image side up, and allow to dry overnight until hard.

4 Fix the images to piped cupcakes, if desired, by moistening the back of the fondant with water, using a pastry brush, and pressing into place.

Variation

You could print icing sheets yourself with lettering and/or images, but to do that you will need a specially adapted printer with edible ink. Alternatively, email your design to a specialist company who will print it for you.

FINISHING TOUCHES

That finishing touch makes all the difference to your cake. From spray-glazing to spinning sugar, the techniques are simple and the results are showstopping. Insert ribbons and fresh flowers, decorate with silver dragées and edible diamonds or gems, and transform your cake or decoration into a work of art.

Working with edible glitter

You can dust cakes with edible glitter dust and make sugar decorations even prettier with edible glitter flakes. You could also add glitter to piping gel or royal icing, to highlight embossed shapes, such as this heart, or to use for piping shimmering lettering.

Equipment

* cutter, to emboss
* piping bag with a round piping tip

Ingredients

* piping gel or royal icing
* edible glitter flakes
* edible glitter dust
* fondant or flower paste plaque, or other decoration

...make sugar decorations prettier with glitter flakes

Variation

Use a small paintbrush to apply edible glue to the surface of a decoration, or onto embossed lines on a decoration or cake, and cover well with a few shakes of glitter flakes or dust. Allow to dry and use a large, soft brush to gently remove any excess.

1 Mix piping gel with the flakes and/or dust, using a paintbrush until you achieve your desired look. Piping gel does not set hard, so for a firmer result, use royal icing instead. Emboss a fondant plaque or decoration with a cookie cutter.

2 Fill a piping bag with a glitter mixture, as prepared above. Pipe into the lines embossed on the plaque or decoration, and allow to set overnight.

Using sugar gems

Adorn your cakes with realistic edible jewels. Keep sugar gems, such as these sugar diamonds, in an airtight container and place them on the cake or decoration at the very last minute, or they will cloud. Use tweezers, rather than your fingers, to apply.

Equipment

* fondant roller
* large plunger cutter
* tweezers

Ingredients

* cornflour, for dusting
* strengthened fondant (see p87)
* cupcakes piped with buttercream icing
* royal icing (see pp34–35)
* large sugar diamonds

...place realistic edible jewels on your cakes at the last minute

1 Dust a surface with cornflour and roll out the fondant to the desired thickness. Use a plunger cutter to cut out shapes, such as these daisies. Allow to dry until just beginning to harden.

2 Moisten the back of each shape with water and apply to the top of your cake. Place a small amount of royal icing in the centre of each daisy, and top with a sugar diamond.

Inserting ribbons

This technique works best on a cake that has been covered completely with fondant and left to rest for at least one day. Make sure you have enough ribbon to wrap all the way around the cake. You could easily insert ribbons onto the top of your cake, too.

Equipment

* knife with flat-ended blade
* tweezers
* ribbon, cut into 1cm (½in) lengths

Ingredients

* fondant-covered cake

Variations

For edible alternatives, you can create ribbons with flower paste (see pp118–19) and insert them carefully while they are still soft and pliable. You could also cut printed icing sheets (see pp150–51) into ribbons and insert those.

1 Use the knife to make small cuts in the fondant covering, about 2.5cm (1in) from the base. Cut the slots in pairs, about 5mm (¼in) wide and 1cm (½in) apart. Make sure the length of each slot is slightly longer than the width of the ribbon.

2 Use the tweezers to carefully insert one end of a ribbon piece into the top slot. Curve the ribbon downwards and feed the other end into the lower slot. Repeat around the base of the cake until all the slots are filled with ribbon. Gently smooth down the pieces of ribbon with your fingers.

Quilting and adding dragées

Quilting produces an embossed pattern, and is great for novelty designs, such as handbag cakes. Use a stitching tool and a printed mat to help you achieve a neat, regular pattern. You could press dragées (hard sugar balls with a metallic sugar coating) into the quilted corners.

Equipment

* fondant mat, marked with squares or diamonds
* fondant roller
* stitching (quilting) tool
* icing scraper or ruler to use for a straight edge
* 5cm (2in) circle cutter
* tweezers

Ingredients

* cornflour, for dusting
* fondant
* fondant-covered cake, decorated with ribbon, if desired
* silver dragées

Tip
You could use royal icing to attach dragées more securely. Work quickly – it hardens fast, making it difficult for the dragées to stick. If you find this tricky, try adding a dot of piping gel to the royal icing – this will keep it moist for longer.

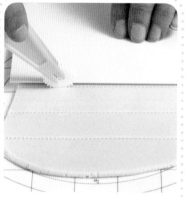

1 Dust the mat with cornflour and roll out the fondant. Score a series of lines using the stitching tool and the edge of a scraper.

2 Using the scraper, score a series of vertical lines into the fondant. Ensure that the gap between each line is the same.

3 Cut out a circle of fondant, using the cutter. Lift it over the cake with a palette knife. Smooth down carefully.

4 Press dragées onto the quilted circle using tweezers. Cover a whole crumb-coated cake with the quilted fondant, if preferred.

Crimping

Crimpers are small tools, like tongs, with patterned edges. They are used to imprint patterns on fondant-covered cake drums, cakes, or decorations. The rubber bands on the arms determine the width of the pattern imprinted on the cake. Use crimpers while the fondant is still soft.

Equipment

* crimper
* pure bristle pastry brush

Ingredients

* fondant-covered cake drum or cake
* lustre dust

...imprint patterns on fondant-covered cake drums and cakes

Tips

All lustre dusts can be mixed with rejuvenator spirit or vodka to make an edible paint (see p136). Mix pearl and petal or blossom dusts to create a tinted, gentle shine. Knead dusts into fondant or molten white chocolate for a hint of sparkle.

1 Position the crimper at a 90° angle above the surface of the cake drum. Press halfway into the fondant, but not all the way through to the drum. Gently squeeze, and then release the arms.

2 Carefully remove the crimper from the fondant and repeat the technique until you have the desired look. Take care not to remove the crimper before you release the pressure, or you will damage the fondant. Using the pastry brush, apply the lustre dust.

Spinning sugar

Spun sugar can produce a variety of different decorative touches. Use it to create smoke for a chimney, a nest for sugar birds or eggs, or a spider's web. Brushing the pan with cold water prevents the sugar from crystallizing. Spun sugar hardens in minutes, so work quickly.

Equipment

* pure bristle pastry brush
* sugar thermometer

Ingredients

* 250g (9oz) caster sugar
* 240ml (8fl oz) water

...create smoke, delicate nests, or a spider's web

Variation

To make spun-sugar trees, add a few drops of green colouring paste to the sugar and water before you heat them. Follow the method up to step 3, then gently press the sugar strands into a cone shape around a cake-pop stick. Allow to harden.

1 Gently heat the sugar and water in a heavy-based pan. Do not stir. Dip a brush in cold water and brush the sides of the pan.

2 Continue to cook the mixture until it reaches 155°C (311°F). Take the pan off the heat and plunge into a bowl of water.

3 Dip a fork into the syrup, then quickly whip the syrup back and forth over a rolling pin to create strands.

4 Gather the strands with your hands and shape as desired. Place on baking parchment to cool and harden completely.

Spraying with mists and glazes

Finish off cakes with a beautiful, edible colour mist spray. You can use a variety of solid colours to spray the surface of your cakes – these also come in metallic or pearlescent finishes. A clear spray glaze can also be used to provide sheen and highlights.

Equipment

* tweezers, optional

Ingredients

* fondant-covered cakes
* colour mist spray
* clear spray glaze
* royal icing (see pp34–35)
* silver dragées, optional

Use a lustre spray for a metallic or pearlescent coating

Tip

You can use spray glaze, also known as confectioner's spray, to add shine to chocolate that may get marked with fingerprints. Spray glazes are preferable to brushed glazes, as they offer an even finish that only takes moments to dry.

1 Place the cakes on a sheet of baking parchment to protect the work surface and allow you to move them easily after spraying.

2 Shake the spray can, and hold it about 15cm (6in) away from the cake. Lightly mist over the surface for a subtle tint.

3 Allow to dry and then spray with glaze for a uniform, shiny appearance. Decorate as soon as the glaze is dry.

To add dragées, dot royal icing around the base of each cake at regular intervals. Using tweezers, press a dragée into each dot.

Displaying sugar flowers

You can adorn cakes with sugar flowers using a little royal icing. However, if you want to attach flower sprays, you will need to use flower picks as a safety measure. Group the sprays, sticking them into florist oasis, to design the bouquet you want before affixing to the cake.

Equipment
* cake drum or board
* turntable or lazy Susan
* food-safe flower picks

Ingredients
* fondant-covered or iced cake
* flower paste or fondant flowers and foliage, on wires (see pp88–89)
* edible glue, optional
* clear glaze spray, optional

Variation
To create a bouquet, start with leaves at the bottom. Put the large flowers in the centre, then add the rest of the flowers and foliage. Wrap the stems with a length of fondant ribbon and a bow. Lightly brush the top of the cake with water and lay the bouquet on top.

1 Place the cake and its drum on the turntable. Put the largest flower in a flower pick and insert it into the top of the cake edge.

2 Select some smaller flowers and place them in a flower pick. Arrange them on the cake so that all the wires are covered.

3 Continue to add flowers, filling the gaps. Add the foliage, popping the wires into flower picks and repeating the process.

4 If desired, give the flower display a light spray with clear glaze spray (see p159) to seal and add shine.

Displaying fresh flowers

Fresh flowers have a striking impact and can give a sense of the season to your cake designs. Edible flowers, such as roses, pansies, and lilac, are the perfect choice. Never push flower stems directly into the cake; use flower picks instead.

Equipment

* secateurs or scissors
* turntable or lazy Susan
* food-safe flower picks
* piping bag and tip, optional

Ingredients

* fresh flowers (edible, if desired) soaked in tepid water for 1 hour
* fondant-covered or iced cake
* chocolate or other flavoured buttercream icing (see pp24–25)

Variation

You can use a florist oasis soaked in water and a plastic plate to create a display on your cake. Fix the plate to the top of the cake with buttercream and place the oasis on top. Push a dowel through the oasis, plate, and cake. Press flower stems into the oasis.

1 Pat the flowers dry and cut stems to the desired length. Place the cake on the turntable so that you can access all sides easily. Fill the flower picks with a little water and press the stem of a flower into each one.

2 One-by-one, press the picks into the sides of the cake at a downward angle, so the picks cannot be seen. Continue around the cake until you have a uniform ring of flowers. Pipe a little chocolate buttercream over any places where the picks are evident. Mist with a light spray of water.

PROJECTS

Create a stunning array of celebration cakes for virtually any occasion. Step-by-step instructions and helpful tips ensure success. Whether you want to decorate a cake for a wedding, child's birthday party, or Christmas celebration, you'll find everything you need for the cake of your dreams – as well as many, many ideas for more.

Train cake

This cheeky train is covered in painted smooth blue fondant, with flower-paste and fondant features glued into place with a little water. Let loose on his edible track, he'll be sure to please a crowd of little ones.

 **TIMING** allow 1½ days, including drying time

 **SERVES** 25

Equipment

* ❋ fondant roller
* ❋ 35cm (14in) round cake drum
* ❋ woodwork texture sheet
* ❋ multi-ribbon cutter
* ❋ circle cutters: 6cm (2¼in), 7cm (2¾in), 4.5cm (1¾in), and 4cm (1½in)
* ❋ veining tool
* ❋ round piping tip (such as PME no. 1)
* ❋ 1m (3ft) green satin ribbon (1cm/½in wide)
* ❋ craft glue

1 Two days before serving, roll out the lime green fondant on a cornflour-dusted surface and cover the drum (see p51), leaving a 10cm (4in) gap for the tracks. Strengthen 100g (3½oz) of the black fondant, roll it out, and cut a strip to fit into the gap. Roll out the grey fondant, and then cut 2 strips, 2.5cm (1in) wide. Place on the black fondant as rails. Roll out the brown fondant and emboss with the texture sheet. Cut 10 strips, 2 x 10cm (¾ x 4in) in size. Moisten and place across the track, as slats. Set aside to dry.

2 Strengthen 200g (7oz) of the yellow fondant (see p87), and roll it out to 4mm (⅙in) thick. Use the cutters to cut four 6cm (2¼in) circles and two 7cm (2¾in) circles. Cut the sheet of flower paste into fine strips with the ribbon cutter and fix to the circles as spokes. Cut 6 more strips, wider than the depth of the circles, and fix them around the wheels. Allow to dry overnight.

3 Halve the cake, to make two 12.5cm (5in) slabs. Halve one of those slabs, to make two 6.5cm (2½in) pieces. Sandwich the smaller pieces together with buttercream and fix on top of the large slab to create the cabin. Freeze until just firm, and then carve the top of the tall end into a gentle curve. Crumb coat the whole cake with buttercream (see p29), and allow to set for 30 minutes.

BRING IT ALL TOGETHER

Using multi-ribbon cutters see p118

Using cookie cutters see pp106–07

Carving and covering cakes see p65

Ingredients

* cornflour, for dusting
* 400g (14oz) lime green fondant, strengthened
* tylose powder
* 200g (7oz) black fondant
* 100g (3½oz) grey fondant, strengthened
* 150g (5½oz) brown fondant, strengthened
* 400g (14oz) yellow fondant
* 75g (2½oz) sheet of black flower paste
* 25cm (10in) Madeira cake, 7.5cm (3in) deep
* 400g (14oz) buttercream
* 600g (1lb 5oz) blue fondant
* 400g (14oz) red fondant
* edible black dust
* superwhite icing whitener
* rejuvenator spirit or vodka
* 75g (2½oz) white fondant

Tip

To make the cow-catcher at the front, strengthen the white fondant and form into a block. Use a knife to cut a shape that is triangular in front, with a flat top and sides. Moisten it with water, and cover the white shape with yellow fondant.

4 On a cornflour-dusted surface, roll out the blue fondant to 4mm (⅙in) thick. Cover the cake and transfer it to the cake drum. Decorate the front of the train with 2 black fondant strips (1.5 x 6cm/⅔ x 2¼in). Strengthen the remaining blue fondant, and roll out a thick cylinder, 7cm (2¾in) wide. Moisten the base and fix to the train. Decorate it with 4 evenly spaced strips (1cm/½in wide) and a 4.5cm (1¾in) circle of red fondant. Cut a long strip of red fondant (4cm/1½in wide) to fix around the base of the train. Attach this, then fix the wheels on top.

5 Strengthen and roll out the remaining red fondant to 4mm (⅙in) thick. Cut a rectangle about 4mm (⅙in) wider than the curved top of the train's cabin. Allow it to firm up for 20 minutes, and then fix it to the cake to form the cabin roof. Roll together the excess red fondant and model into a cone shape for the chimney, about 4cm (1½in) wide at the base and 5cm (2in) tall. Cut off each end to get a flat top and bottom. Decorate with a strip of blue fondant and a circle of yellow fondant. Set aside.

6 Cut a 4cm (1½in) circle from yellow fondant, score a smile with a veining tool, and fix to the front. Use a piping tip to cut 8 small circles from the yellow fondant, and fix these to the centre of the wheels, and to the front of the cabin. Mark the windows on either side of the cabin and a curved window on the front with a sharp knife. Mix together black edible dust and a little superwhite icing whitener with rejuvenator spirit, and paint the windows. Allow each to dry and then edge with thin strips of black fondant.

7 Cut a base for the chimney out of black fondant and fix to its base, then stick the entire chimney to the train. Emboss the top with the 4.5cm (1¾in) cutter. Fix a tiny circle of black fondant above the smile, and create the eyes (see Tip, p166).

8 Model the cow-catcher (see Tip, left) and fix it to the front of the train. To decorate it, roll out some red fondant, and cut 11 thin strips. Apply one to the centre of the cow-catcher, and fix on the rest at even intervals. Trim with black fondant.

9 Strengthen the remaining blue fondant and roll out to 2mm (1/16in) thick. Cut 2 strips, 1cm (½in) wide, and 17cm (6¾in) long. Allow them to dry for 20 minutes, and then fix them across both sets of wheels. Glue the ribbon around the cake drum.

Tip

To create the eyes for the train, cut 2 eye shapes from some rolled fondant, and fix to the window. Mix together a little black dust with rejuvenator spirit and paint the pupils. Dab flecks of superwhite and rejuvenator spirit to create the gleam.

Train cake pp164–65

Dinosaur cake pp168–69

Dinosaur cake

Crouched on a marbled board dotted with fondant rocks, this fierce little dinosaur will delight younger children. The cake is made using two bowl-shaped sponges (see Tip), then carved and covered with tinted fondant.

 **TIMING** allow 1½ days, including drying time

 **SERVES** 30

Equipment

* fondant roller
* 35cm (14in) cake drum
* veining tool
* ball tool
* 1m (3ft) stone-coloured satin ribbon (1cm/½in wide)
* craft glue

Ingredients

* 600g (1lb 5oz) white fondant (reserve 25g/ scant 1oz)
* tylose powder
* 200g (7oz) chocolate brown fondant
* cornflour, for dusting

1 A day before you wish to serve the cake, strengthen the white fondant with a little tylose powder, kneading it in well (see p87). Marble it with the chocolate brown fondant (see p47), carefully roll it out on a cornflour-dusted surface, and cover the cake drum (see p51). Set aside to harden for a day.

2 Place the smaller bowl cake in the freezer and, when firm, carve into the head shape. Crumb coat it in buttercream icing (see p29). Apply strips of gooseberry-green fondant around the eyes and nose, to build up these areas. Set aside for about 30 minutes, or until the buttercream icing has just set.

3 Place the large cake upside down, and crumb coat with buttercream icing. Strengthen a length of gooseberry-green fondant (see p87) and form into a cone shape, for the tail.

4 Roll out the remaining gooseberry-green fondant on a cornflour-dusted surface to 4mm (⅙in) thick, and cover the head and body, working from the top to the bottom. Smooth downwards as you go. Cut off any excess and press the edges under the base of the body with the back of a knife. Join the tail to the body and smooth the join with your fingers. Transfer the

BRING IT ALL TOGETHER

Covering a cake drum *see p51*

Carving and covering cakes *see p65*

Dusting with edible dust *see p136*

* 750ml (1¼ pints) bowl cake, in vanilla sponge (see p228)
* 400g (14oz) buttercream icing, to crumb coat (see p29)
* 1.5kg (3lb 3oz) gooseberry-green fondant
* 1 litre (1¾ pints) bowl cake, in vanilla sponge (see p228)
* 12g (½oz) pale blue fondant
* 12g (½oz) black fondant
* confectioner's glaze
* 75g (2½oz) pale gooseberry-green fondant
* moss-green edible petal dust
* 200g (7oz) grey fondant

Tip

Baking a cake in a Pyrex (or pudding) bowl involves the same steps as baking half of a ball cake (see p237). You need to insert a heat conductor, such as a slim, short skewer, into the centre of the batter before it is baked, to ensure that it bakes evenly.

dinosaur to the covered cake drum. Use the veining tool to tuck under the edges, and your fingers to smooth the fondant where it meets the cake drum.

5 Use the veining tool to mark an incision that will become the mouth. Use the ball tool to create nostrils and to create ellipse-shaped sockets for the eyes.

6 Strengthen the remaining gooseberry-green fondant and form 4 legs, using about 200g (7oz) of fondant per leg. Make a tapered sausage for each leg. Flatten the narrower end for the foot, and use a sharp knife to cut 3 toes into the end of each. Press each foot upwards and score the ankles and the upper thighs with the veining tool, to give a wrinkled effect. Moisten the thigh-end of the legs with some water, and attach them to the base of the body, curving the legs slightly outwards.

7 Strengthen the reserved white fondant (see p87) and use your hands to model 2 rounded ellipses with pointed sides, to fit into the eye sockets. Moisten the back of the eyes with some water and press into the sockets, allowing them to bulge out. Cut 2 irises from the pale blue fondant and press into place. Cut 2 strips of black fondant, moisten the backs, and fix to the eyes for the pupils. Brush with 2 coats of confectioner's glaze.

8 Strengthen the pale gooseberry-green fondant (see p87), and form into 11 cones in descending sizes, using your fingers. Flatten and then cut off the widest end to create a flat edge on each. Roll one into a horn for the nose and curve it backwards slightly. Allow to dry for 20 minutes, and then moisten the base of each and fix onto the head and spine of the dinosaur.

9 Using a larger brush, dust the body with moss-green edible petal dust, guiding the brush into all the crevices, to add depth and texture. Use the veining tool to create more ridges, if required.

10 Knead the grey fondant and, using your hands, form into different shaped rocks. Dot around the covered cake drum.

11 Cut a length of ribbon to fit around the circumference of the cake drum, and fix it into place with craft glue, making sure that the join is at the back.

Princess castle

This castle cake is the ideal centrepiece for a fairy-tale party. The base cake is layered with fondant shapes to create an idyllic backdrop, and an exquisite hand-carved and modelled castle sits on top. Finish it off with a little princess (see pp92–93), complete with crown.

 **TIMING** allow 4 days, including drying time

 **SERVES** 25

Equipment

* fondant roller
* 35cm (14in) round cake drum
* frilling tool
* piping bag with fine tip (such as PME no. 0)
* sheet of cardboard
* masking tape
* cutting wheel
* 2 fondant smoothers
* 23cm (9in) round cake board

1 Four days before you wish to serve the cake, dust a flat surface with cornflour, roll out the leaf-green fondant, and use to cover the cake drum (see p51). Set aside to dry for 4 days.

For the princess

2 Model the basic figure on pp92–93. Cut out a small heart from pink fondant and stick it to the centre of her bodice. Use the frilling tool to form curls in her hair. Make the crown by rolling out a piece of leftover fondant, and cutting out the shape with a sharp knife. Dry in shape and then paint with gold lustre dust mixed with rejuvenator spirit. Pipe beads of royal icing on the tips of the crown, and fix to the hair with edible glue.

For the castle

3 Create a forming cone for the large turret (see Tip, opposite). Grease the outside of the cone lightly with white vegetable fat.

METHOD CONTINUES • • • •

BRING IT ALL TOGETHER

Modelling a basic figure see pp92-93

Creating strong 3D objects see p64

Making a template see p57

Building tiered cakes see p68

Tip

To make a forming cone, cut out a 23cm (9in) circle from cardboard. Make a single cut from one edge of the circle to the centre. Form a cone approximately 12.5cm (5in) in diameter at the base. Fix with masking tape and trim the base of the cone.

* 12.5cm (5in) round cake board
* circle cutters, 4.5cm (1¾in), 5mm (¼in), and 1cm (½in) in diameter
* 8 dowels
* template for base cake design (see pp244–45)
* blossom plunger cutter, small
* heart-shaped plunger cutters, small, medium, large, and extra large
* multi-ribbon cutter, straight and wavy edges
* 1m (3ft) pink satin ribbon (1cm/½in wide)
* craft glue

Ingredients

* cornflour, for dusting
* 1kg (2¼lb) leaf-green fondant
* edible gold lustre dust
* rejuvenator spirit or vodka
* royal icing, for piping (see p35)
* edible glue
* white vegetable fat
* icing sugar, for dusting
* 500g (1lb 2oz) pink Mexican paste (see p53)
* 1.5kg (3lb 3oz) pale blue fondant
* 23cm (9in) 2-layer Madeira cake (see p231),

4 Dust a flat surface with icing sugar, and roll out the pink Mexican paste. Using a cutting wheel, cut a 23cm (9in) circle and, as with the card, cut a single straight line from the edge to the centre of the circle. Working quickly, carefully lift the paste onto the cardboard cone and draw one edge over the other. Trim off any excess paste, allowing a 6mm (¼in) overlap. Fix in place with edible glue. Leave to dry for at least 3 days.

5 Roll out the pale blue fondant to 4mm (⅛in) thick on a cornflour-dusted surface and cover the 23cm (9in) cake, using the fondant smoother to achieve a smooth surface (see p50). Place on the 23cm (9in) board and allow to dry overnight.

6 Using a very wide palette knife, transfer the iced cake to the covered cake drum, placing it towards the back to leave space in the front for the princess and mini cupcakes, if desired.

7 Roll out the ivory fondant. Place the 12.5cm (5in) cake on its board and use the fondant to cover the cake, using 2 fondant smoothers to get a sharp, crisp top edge (see p50).

8 Use a 4.5cm (1¾in) circle cutter to cut 20 circles from the slab of Madeira cake. Sandwich each with buttercream icing, and create 4 towers, each a little over 12.5cm (5in) in height. Set them next to the small ivory cake to measure them – they should be exactly the same height as the fondant-covered cake on its board. Trim if necessary.

9 Insert a dowel into the centre of each tower, laying them on their sides so that the dowel pokes out from the top and bottom. Crumb coat the towers with buttercream icing (see p29). Roll out the remaining ivory fondant and cover the towers by wrapping strips around the outside, and then fitting a circle of fondant to the top. Smooth the sides and the top for a crisp edge. Trim the dowels and lay the towers on a flat surface dusted with icing sugar, join sides down. Dry overnight.

10 Roll out the remaining strengthened leaf-green fondant (used to cover the cake drum). Using the template, cut a wavy background pattern that will fit around the cake, with a gap at the front for the castle steps, and then loosely roll it up. Apply to the cake with a little water, using the cake drum to support the fondant roll as you unwind it and press it onto the cake.

filled and crumb coated with buttercream icing (see p29), about 7.5cm (3in) in height

* 1.5kg (3lb 3oz) ivory fondant
* 12.5cm (5in) 2-layer vanilla sponge cake (see p228), filled and crumb coated with buttercream icing (see p28), about 12.5cm (5in) in height
* 1 slab of Madeira cake (see p231), 2.5cm (1in) thick
* 100g (3½oz) buttercream icing (see pp24–25)
* 75g (2½oz) each of 4–5 shades of green fondant, strengthened (see p87)
* 50g (1¾oz) each of pink, fuchsia, yellow, lilac, brown, and red fondant, strengthened (see p87)
* 500g (1lb 2oz) white fondant, strengthened (see p87)
* 200g (7oz) fuchsia fondant, strengthened (see p87)
* 500g (1lb 2oz) pink fondant, strengthened (see p87)
* 300g (10oz) lilac fondant

For the garden

11 Use the template to cut shapes from the various shades of strengthened green fondant (reserve the darkest green for the trees), to create a patchwork effect of fields. Create striped fields by laying thin strips of pale fondant over darker fondant, and rolling them out together. Work around the cake, piecing together the field landscape neatly.

12 Roll out the pink, fuchsia, yellow, and lilac fondants, one at a time, and use the blossom plunger cutter to cut out lots of tiny blossoms. Provide each with a centre of fondant in a contrasting colour. Moisten the back of some flowers with a little water and fix to the cake. Put the others aside to decorate the board when the cake is finished.

13 Create trees by moulding small trunks (about 1.5cm/⅔in high) and larger trunks (about 2cm/¾in high) from strengthened brown fondant. Scratch with a knife to look like bark, then moisten the reverse, and fix to the cake. Roll out the darkest green fondant and use heart-shaped plunger cutters to create 2 sizes of tree tops. Fix to the cake above the trunks. Cut out small hearts and circles from rolled red fondant, and fix to the tree tops with a little water.

METHOD CONTINUES • • • •

Princess mini cupcakes
Pipe cupcakes with buttercream icing and top them with tiaras, cut from thin strengthened fondant. Allow to dry and pipe beads on each tip. Paint them with silver dust. Fix on fondant hearts with water.

14 Roll out the white fondant, and cut out a cloud shape. It should be wide and long enough for the castle, including all 4 turrets, to sit comfortably on top, fanning out towards the steps at the front of the cake. Moisten the back of the cloud with a little water and fix to the top of the base cake. Smooth the edges to soften.

15 Form the remaining white fondant into a ball and then, using a knife, cut out a flight of stairs that will sit against the cake at the front. The stairs should be high enough to meet the trailing piece of cloud, about three-quarters of the way up the side of the cake. Cut a smaller cloud shape with the excess, and fix it to the covered cake drum, directly in the centre. It should be wide enough for the princess to sit on top. Fix the stairs to the front of the cake with some edible glue.

To bring it all together

16 Place 4 dowels into the base cake, using the 12.5cm (5in) cake base as a guide. Cut to height and place the ivory cake on top.

17 Place the towers around the cake as evenly as possible, using royal icing to secure the towers to the base cake and the sides of the ivory cake, ensuring that all the joins are facing inwards. Press the dowels down into the base cake a little.

18 Roll out the ivory fondant on a cornflour-dusted surface and cut out a rectangle shape that narrows slightly at one end. It should be a little more than 12.5cm (5in) in height, and fit neatly onto the front of the cake to form the entrance. Fix into place with a little water.

19 Cut a heart-shaped door from the strengthened fuchsia fondant and score with vertical lines. Cut 2 tiny lilac hearts to make door handles and fix to the door. Attach the door to the cake with a little water. Roll out the strengthened yellow fondant and cut 4 small triangles, to create the hinges. Fix to the sides of the door, and paint with gold dust mixed with rejuvenator spirit. Roll out more fuchsia fondant on a cornflour-dusted surface and cut 12 hearts using the plunger cutters: 4 small, 4 medium, and 4 large. Fix these to the towers with water, to create windows.

20 Lift the dried roof from the cardboard cone and place on top of the central ivory cake, placing the join at the back. Secure the roof with royal icing. Form a small ball of pink fondant and place it on the roof. Cut out 6 large fuchsia hearts, using the plunger cutter. Fix 1 to the front of the roof and another on top of the pink fondant ball on top. Model a fuchsia bow, and fix it to the roof under the fondant ball with some water.

Tip
Use pastillage, flower paste, or strengthened fondant instead of Mexican paste; but these may require extra time to dry thoroughly, ideally in a dry place, such as an airing cupboard. You could use polystyrene cylinders instead of cake for the turrets.

21 Make 4 balls of pink fondant, each weighing about 50g (1¾oz). Dust your hands with some cornflour and form each into a cone-shaped roof, with the base of each cone just over 4.5cm (1¾in) in diameter. Attach to the top of each tower with royal icing. Top each turret with a fuchsia heart.

22 On a surface dusted with cornflour, roll out the strengthened lilac fondant. Using the ribbon cutter, cut a ribbon about 2.5cm (1in) wide and 35cm (14in) long (trim to length when in place). Use a small circle cutter to create a crenellated top edge to the ribbon, and then attach it around the top of the ivory cake with a little water. Cut another piece of ribbon to fit over the entrance, with the crenellated top edge slightly wider than the base, and score the bottom of the ribbon with the back of a knife. Moisten and fix to the top of the entrance.

23 Use a wavy attachment on the ribbon cutter to create the crenellated top edge of the ribbons that will top the towers, and a sharp knife to cut the bottom edge. Cut 4 ribbons in this way, each about 1cm (½in) wide and 17cm (6¾in) long, and fix to the top of the towers, where they meet the roofs.

24 Cover the join at the back of the main roof with a row of tiny hearts, cut from fuchsia fondant and applied with water.

25 Position the princess on the cloud shape on the cake drum, in front of the steps, using royal icing to secure. Dot the remaining blossoms around the board, moistening the backs with a little water to adhere. Trim the cake drum with pink ribbon, adhering with a little craft glue and making sure the join is at the back.

Princess cake pops
Mould cake pops (see p242) into heart shapes before dipping into pink candy melts. Use pink and white royal icing to pipe beads. Dip round pops into green candy melts, allow to dry, and fix on pink fondant hearts with a little water.

Pirate ship cake

Set sail on the seven seas with a spectacular pirate ship, complete with an anchor and skull-and-crossbones sails. Displayed on a fondant wave-encrusted board, this cake is carved from layers of sponge and covered with weather-beaten fondant planks.

 **TIMING** allow 1½ days, including drying time    **SERVES** 40

Equipment

* fondant roller
* multi-ribbon cutter
* circle cutters: 2.5cm (1in), 3cm (1¼in), and 2cm (¾in)
* frilling tool
* 1 wooden dowel
* 2 wooden skewers
* anchor cutter
* 35cm (14in) round cake drum
* white rice paper
* skull and crossbones stencil
* 1m (3ft) navy satin ribbon (1cm/½in wide)

1 A day before you wish to serve, halve your cake so that you have two 12.5 x 25cm (5 x 10in) pieces, each 7.5cm (3in) thick. Carefully cut 1 of these pieces into 2 layers, each 12.5 x 25 x 4cm (5 x 10 x 1½in). Sandwich 1 of the thin layers on top of the thicker piece of cake with some buttercream icing. Take the remaining layer of cake and cut it into 3 equal pieces, 8cm (just over 3in) long and 12.5cm (5in) wide. Sandwich 2 of these together with buttercream icing and fix to one end of the cake with more buttercream icing to make the bow of the ship. Stick the remaining piece of cake to the other end of the cake with buttercream icing, to become the stern. Place the whole cake in the freezer for ½ hour–1 hour, or until just firm.

2 Carve the bow of the ship into a prow-shaped point, using a sharp serrated knife. Carve the sides into a smooth curve towards the back of the ship, and from the top of the deck down to the base with a gentle slope. Carve the steps from the tallest area of the cake for the stern of the ship, using a ruler to ensure that they are level and evenly spaced. Crumb coat the entire cake with buttercream icing (see p29), and leave to set for 30 minutes.

METHOD CONTINUES • • • •

BRING IT ALL TOGETHER

Carving and covering cakes *see p65*

Using multi-ribbon cutters *see p118*

Using cookie cutters *see pp106-07*

Ingredients

* 25cm (10in) square
  Madeira cake (see p231),
  about 7.5cm (3in) deep
* 600g (1lb 5oz) buttercream
  icing (see pp24–25)
* cornflour, for dusting
* 600g (1lb 5oz)
  brown fondant
* 50g (1¾oz) black fondant
* 50g (1¾oz) red fondant,
  strengthened (see p87)
* 100g (3½oz) gold fondant,
  strengthened (see p87)
* dark brown
  colouring paste
* 25g (scant 1oz) grey
  fondant, strengthened
  (see p87)
* 250g (9oz) blue fondant
  and 150g (5½oz) white
  fondant, marbled (see p47)
* superwhite icing whitener
* blue colouring paste
* 50g (1¾oz) brown
  flower paste
* edible black felt-tip pen
* gold and silver edible
  lustre dusts
* rejuvenator spirit
  or vodka

3 Dust a flat surface with cornflour, and roll out some brown fondant to 4mm (⅛in) thick. Use this to cover the top of the ship, including the decks and the stairs. Use a sharp knife to score the surface with long and short floorboards, about 2.5cm (1in). Use your knife to scratch lines and swirls.

4 Roll out the remaining brown fondant, and use the ribbon cutter to cut strips about 2.5cm (1in) wide, in many different lengths. Lightly moisten the back of the strips and place them around the base of the ship, continuing upwards until two-thirds of the ship is covered. Score the surface of the strips with a sharp knife. Use a cocktail stick to poke all 4 corners of each strip to create nail holes.

5 Use the 2.5cm (1in) circle cutter to cut 3 portholes from each side of the ship, just below where the wooden strips end. Remove the cake and fondant and discard. On a cornflour-dusted surface, roll out the black fondant to 2mm (¹⁄₁₆in) thick and cut 6 circles with the same cutter. Moisten the backs of each and insert into the holes created in the ship.

6 Roll out the strengthened red fondant on a cornflour-dusted surface. Cut 6 circles, using the 3cm (1¼in) cutter, and then cut the centre out with the 2.5cm (1in) cutter. Allow to set for 15 minutes and then moisten the back and fix to the cake so that the red circles frame the portholes.

7 Next, roll out the gold fondant on a surface dusted with cornflour. Cut panels to fit the sides and back of the ship, from the panelled brown fondant to the top of the deck, adding about 5mm (¼in) so that it sticks up above the deck a little. You will need 2 panels for the prow, 2 for the lower deck in the centre, 2 that are cut to fit the shape of the stairs, and 1 for the back of the ship. Use the point of the frilling tool to poke holes in the surface of the fondant, to resemble rivets.

8 Press the dowel into the centre of the ship, with 2 skewers either side. Cut to height of sails (see step 12). Mix a little brown colouring paste with water, and paint the skewers. Roll out the grey fondant on a cornflour-dusted surface, and use the cutter for an anchor. Allow to dry for 3 hours.

9 On a cornflour-dusted surface, roll out the marbled blue and white fondant to 6mm (¼in), and cover the cake drum. Place the ship on its centre. Pinch the marbled fondant to create waves over the surface surrounding the ship. Paint the tops of the waves with superwhite icing whitener, and the base with blue colouring paste mixed with water.

10 Roll out a long rope of brown flower paste, about 5mm (¼in) wide, and cut into 18 segments about 3cm (1¼in) long. Allow to dry for 30 minutes and then moisten the ends with water and fix to the front and rear decks to create spindles for the bannister. Measure the length of each bannister and cut out strips of brown flower paste, wider than the spindles. Allow to dry. Fix to the spindles with some water.

11 Using the 2cm (¾in) circle cutter, cut 2 cannon holes from each side of the ship, at the rear, on the gold panels (see opposite) and replace the centres with black fondant circles, as you did in step 5. Roll out the red fondant and cut circular frames to fit around the cannon holes, using the biggest and medium circle cutters. Fix around the holes with water. Cut strips of red fondant, 2mm (⅙in) wide. Moisten the back and fit around the top of the gold panel, to trim. Add rivets to the trim with a frilling tool.

12 Cut the rice paper into a variety of different-sized squares. On the largest sail, place on the stencil and use the black felt-tip edible pen to paint on the image. Cut holes from the centre of the base and the top of each sail, and slide them onto the skewers and the dowel. Take 3 pea-sized balls of brown flower paste and press them down into flat circles. Moisten the base of each and place on top of the "sail posts".

13 Mix together some gold lustre dust with rejuvenator spirit and paint the gold panels. Moisten the back of the dried anchor, and fix it to the side of the boat, near the front. Mix together some silver lustre dust with rejuvenator spirit, and paint the anchor. Trim the cake drum with the ribbon, making sure the join is at the back.

Pirate cake pops
Dip cake pops (see pp242–43) into melted candy melts and decorate with flower-paste eye patches and bandanas. Use a piping tip to cut out white flower-paste circles, and fix them to the top with edible glue. Use edible felt-tip pens for other details. You could form cake crumbs into a parrot shape, dip them into melted green candy melts, and add fondant eyes, a beak, and 3-colour wings, scored with a veining tool.

Soccer ball cake

Decorating this cake is like creating a patchwork quilt. You have to carefully line up the edges of each fondant shape before fixing it to the cake. Although time-consuming to prepare, this cake and the rugby ball cake (see recipe overleaf) will be the crowning glory for anyone who loves sport.

 **TIMING** allow 3-4 days, including drying time    **SERVES** 20

Equipment

* ✻ 33cm (13in) cake drum
* ✻ fondant roller
* ✻ multi-ribbon cutter, straight edges
* ✻ fondant smoother
* ✻ large hexagon and pentagon cutters
* ✻ 1m (3ft) black satin ribbon (1cm/½in wide)
* ✻ craft glue

Ingredients

* ✻ 200g (7oz) green fondant, strengthened (see p87)
* ✻ 200g (7oz) white fondant, strengthened (see p87)
* ✻ cornflour, for dusting
* ✻ edible glue
* ✻ 15cm (6in) Madeira ball cake (see p237)
* ✻ 200g (7oz) buttercream
* ✻ icing sugar, for dusting
* ✻ 600g (1lb 5oz) white fondant
* ✻ 200g (7oz) black fondant

1 Three to four days before you decorate the cake, cover the cake drum (see p51), using the ribbon cutter to cut strips of both green and white strengthened fondant, rolled out to about 3mm (⅛in) thick on a surface dusted with cornflour. Brush the cake drum with edible glue and place alternating colours on top. Smooth down over the edges and surface with the fondant smoother, and cut off excess. Set aside to dry.

2 Place the ball cake on a flat surface and crumb coat it with buttercream icing (see p29). Allow it to set for about 1 hour, and then spread another thin layer of buttercream icing over the surface of the cake, until smooth. On separate surfaces that have been dusted with icing sugar, roll out the black and white fondant to about 3mm (⅛in), ensuring that they are the same thickness.

3 Using the cutters, cut out 5 white hexagons and 5 black pentagons at a time, keeping them covered with cling film while you work. Cover up the excess fondant. Place a black pentagon on the top centre of the ball, fixing it into place with a little extra buttercream icing. Encircle with 5 white hexagons, making sure that the edges meet neatly.

4 Roll out more hexagons and pentagons, and add them to the surface of the ball to create the classic pattern. Gradually build up the shapes to cover the whole ball, turning it over when you have covered the top half. The shapes may need moulding to ensure that they all fit together, so recut any shapes if necessary.

5 When the cake is complete, allow to dry overnight. Carefully move it to the covered cake drum. Secure with buttercream icing. Fix the satin ribbon around the base of the covered cake drum with craft glue. Ensure the join is at the back.

Tips

When carving the rugby ball cake (see p182), it helps to have a photograph in front of you. Better still, print out a ball template (see p245), place it on top of the cake, and then cut the outline using small, even cuts with a serrated knife.

BRING IT ALL TOGETHER

Covering a cake drum
see p51

Using a moulded cake tin see p237

Carving and covering cakes see p65

Rugby ball cake

This hand-carved cake (see p181) is covered in fondant and stitched with a quilting tool. Finish the cake drum with a black ribbon (see p180).

RUGBY BALL CAKE **VARIATION:** BALL GAME MINI CAKES *p183*

 **TIMING** allow 3 days, including drying time

 **SERVES** 20

Equipment

* 33cm (13in) round cake drum
* rugby ball template (see p245)
* fondant roller
* fondant smoother
* stitching (quilting) tool
* multi-ribbon cutter, straight edges

Ingredients

* 200g (7oz) green fondant, strengthened (see p87)
* 300g (10oz) white fondant, strengthened (see p87)
* 25cm (10in) two-layer Madeira cake, sandwiched with buttercream icing
* 200g (7oz) buttercream
* icing sugar, for dusting
* 1kg (2¼lb) brown fondant
* cornflour, for dusting

1 Three days in advance of the celebration, cover the cake drum (see p180, step 1), and set aside to dry. Freeze the cake and place it on a flat surface. Using a sharp, serrated knife and the template, carve in the shape of a rugby ball. Once carved, crumb coat with a little buttercream icing and allow to settle for 1 hour. Smooth another thin coat of buttercream icing over the crumb-coated surface. Refrigerate to firm, for about 1 hour.

2 Place on a firm surface and tidy with a sharp knife. Moisten the surface of the cake with a little water on a pastry brush. Dust a flat surface with icing sugar, and roll out the brown fondant to 5mm (¼in) thick and large enough to wrap around the ball-shaped cake. Lift onto the ball and smooth with your hands.

3 Gather the fondant together under the points at each end of the ball, and trim off the excess. Rub cornflour onto the cut marks, ensuring they remain on the underside of the ball. Smooth down with the fondant smoother. Using the stitching tool, mark 4 evenly spaced horizontal seams on the ball, from one pointed end to the other, taking care not to score through to the cake.

4 Roll out the remaining white fondant on a surface dusted with cornflour to 2mm (¹⁄₁₆in) thick, and use the ribbon cutter to cut out strips, long enough to wrap around the ball. Cut a single thin strip for the central stitching on the ball and 8 smaller strips to fix onto this. Use a little water to fix into place.

5 Move the cake onto the covered cake drum, and secure with buttercream icing. Finish the board with a ribbon (see p180).

RUGBY BALL CAKE **VARIATION**

Ball game mini cakes

Celebrate sport with some clever mini cakes, each adorned with a stencilled ball on top. You can top them with virtually any type of ball to please the crowds. You could use an icing scraper to help remove excess icing when you are stencilling the cakes. Follow more tips on stencilling on pp125–31.

 **TIMING** 2½ hrs    **MAKES** 12

Equipment

* fondant roller
* circle cutters, 15cm (6in) and 5cm (2in) diameter
* 12 x 7.5cm (3in) round cake boards
* fondant smoother
* 3 x sports ball stencils
* 2m (6ft) black ribbon, 1.5cm (⅔in) wide

Ingredients

* icing sugar, for dusting
* 2kg (4½lb) white fondant
* 12 mini Madeira cakes (see p231), 5cm (2in) wide and 3.5cm (1⅓in) high, crumb coated with buttercream (see p29)
* tylose powder
* 100g (3½oz) royal icing (see p34), in black, red, and white
* 50g (1¾oz) orange fondant, strengthened (see p87)

1 On a surface dusted with icing sugar, roll out the white fondant to 5mm (¼in) thick. Cut 12 circles using the large cutter. Use them to cover each cake. Trim off any excess. Dot a little buttercream icing on each cake board, and place the covered cakes on top. Shape the tops with the fondant smoother.

2 Strengthen the remaining white fondant with tylose powder (see p87), and roll it to 3mm (⅛in) thick. Use a knife to cut out 8 squares, 6cm (2¼in) in size. Place the football stencil on one and spread black royal icing over the top. Peel off the stencil and repeat on 3 more squares. Stencil 4 baseballs using the red royal icing. Cut out 4 squares from orange fondant rolled to the same thickness, and stencil white icing basketballs on top.

3 Use the smaller cutter to cut a disc around each ball. Dab each cake with a little water, and carefully place a design on each. Trim the cakes with ribbon, secured with royal icing.

Butterflies and blossoms

These charming cupcakes are spread with rich vanilla buttercream icing, topped with pretty pink fondant butterflies, and nestled in delicate lace cupcake wraps. Serve alongside delightful piped peach cupcakes with a simple yet elegant blossom on top.

 **TIMING** allow 1½ days, including drying time

 **MAKES** 12

Equipment

* fondant roller
* butterfly plunger cutters, medium and small
* blossom plunger cutter, medium
* piping bag with large open star tip (such as Wilton no. 1M)
* lace cupcake wrappers

Ingredients

* cornflour, for dusting
* 200g (7oz) pink fondant, strengthened (see p87)
* 200g (7oz) white fondant, strengthened (see p87)
* 12 cupcakes (see p240)
* 1kg (2¼lb) buttercream icing (see p24), half coloured with peach colouring paste (see pp24–25)

1 A day before you wish to serve the cupcakes, on a flat surface dusted with cornflour, roll out the strengthened pink fondant to about 1mm (¹⁄₁₆in) thick. Use plunger cutters to cut out 10 medium and 10 small butterflies. Bend gently in the centre, and place along the crease of an open book lined with baking parchment to dry in shape overnight.

2 Roll out the strengthened white fondant on a surface dusted with cornflour to about 1mm (¹⁄₁₆in) thick, and use the blossom plunger cutter to cut out 10 blossoms. Place on baking parchment to dry overnight.

3 Using the cone method (see p33), fill the cooled cupcakes with buttercream icing. Using a palette knife, spread uncoloured buttercream icing on 6 cupcakes.

4 Fill the piping bag with peach buttercream icing and attach the open star tip. Pipe the remaining cupcakes.

5 Moisten the back of each dried blossom with water and press gently onto the piped cupcakes. Moisten the back of each butterfly and press onto the surface of the smooth-iced cupcakes. Slip the cupcakes into the lace wrappers and arrange on a stand.

BRING IT ALL TOGETHER

Using plunger cutters
see pp101-03

Filling cupcakes
see p33

Piping cupcakes
see p32

Halloween pumpkin cake

This spooky jack o'lantern cake is carved from a rich Madeira cake, covered in orange fondant, and carefully scored to resemble a real Halloween pumpkin. Cover the cake drum with strengthened purple fondant at least a day before you start decorating.

HALLOWEEN PUMPKIN CAKE **VARIATION:** SCARY CAKE POPS *p189*

 **TIMING** allow ½ day, including drying time

 **SERVES** 25

Equipment

* ✳ fondant roller
* ✳ star plunger cutter
* ✳ 33cm (13in) fondant-covered round cake drum (see p51)
* ✳ veining tool
* ✳ set of triangle cutters
* ✳ ball tool
* ✳ skewers
* ✳ 1m (3ft) black satin ribbon (1cm/½in wide)
* ✳ craft glue

1 On a surface dusted with cornflour, roll out the gold fondant to about 1mm (¹⁄₁₆in) thick, and cut out about 12 stars using the plunger cutter. Moisten the back of each star with water and stick them onto the covered cake drum with edible glue. Set aside to dry.

2 On a surface dusted with cornflour, knead the orange fondant and form into 6 sausage shapes that are long enough to extend from the top of the cake to the base, and about 5cm (2in) wide. Moisten the backs of the sausages and press them onto the sides of the crumb-coated ball cake at even intervals, to add definition and build up the shape.

3 Roll out the remaining orange fondant to about 4mm (¹⁄₆in) thick, so it is large enough to cover the ball and the sausage-shaped fondant detailing. Cover the ball, pushing the fondant into the grooves between the sausages. Dust your hands

METHOD CONTINUES · · · ·

BRING IT ALL TOGETHER

Using a moulded cake tin *see p237*

Using cookie cutters *see pp106–07*

Using edible dusts *see p136*

Ingredients

* cornflour, for dusting
* 50g (1¾oz) gold fondant, strengthened (see p87)
* edible glue
* 700g (1½lb) orange fondant
* 15cm (6in) Madeira ball cake (see p231), levelled and crumb coated with buttercream icing (see p29)
* 50g (1¾oz) black fondant
* 50g (1¾oz) green fondant, strengthened (see p87)
* edible gold lustre dust

with cornflour to smooth down further. Gather the fondant around the base of the cake and cut off any excess, smoothing down. Move the cake to the covered cake drum.

4 Use the veining tool to score the surface of the pumpkin, in a downward motion. Use the triangle cutters to cut out eyes and a nose from the front of the pumpkin and carefully remove the fondant. Use a sharp knife to cut out a mouth shape, and remove the fondant.

5 On a surface dusted with cornflour, roll out the black fondant to about 2mm (¹⁄₁₆in) thick, and cut out triangles and a mouth shape, the same size as the shapes on the pumpkin. Moisten the backs of each with a little water and press into the cut-outs on the pumpkin. Smooth down with your fingers.

6 To model the stalk, form a ball of strengthened green fondant and roll into a thick sausage with your hands. Press it down onto a hard surface dusted with cornflour so that the top is flattened and the bottom begins to fan out. Use a ball tool to smooth out the bottom edges and expand them outwards. Use a veining tool to score the surface.

7 Cut a circle from the orange fondant at the top of the pumpkin. Moisten the base of the stalk and press into place in the circle. Use the veining tool and/or the ball tool to press the orange fondant upwards, over the edges of the base of the stalk so it looks realistic.

8 Roll out thin ropes of strengthened green fondant and cut to different lengths. Dust the skewers with a little cornflour. Wrap the ropes of green fondant around the skewers, and leave for 10 minutes for them to start to set and hold their shape. Remove from the skewers and attach to the pumpkin stalk and the board with a little water.

9 Dust the stars with a little gold lustre dust. Fix the ribbon around the base of the cake drum with a little craft glue, placing the join at the back.

Tips

If you cannot purchase fondant in the desired colours, use food colouring paste, bearing in mind that the final shade will be darker once the colour has set. You could use leftover fondant to create tiny pumpkins to decorate a table.

HALLOWEEN PUMPKIN CAKE **VARIATION**

Scary cake pops

These festive lantern, spooky black cat, and witch's hat cake pops are the ideal treats for a Halloween party. Make a few batches to delight trick-or-treaters, and stand them upright for a striking centrepiece. When modelling your shapes, be sure to wrap excess fondant in cling film for future use.

 **TIMING** allow 1 day, including drying time

 **MAKES** 24

Equipment

* fondant roller
* circle cutter, 5cm (2in)
* 24 cake-pop sticks

Ingredients

* 25g (scant 1oz) yellow fondant
* green colouring paste
* tylose powder
* cornflour, for dusting
* 100g (3½oz) black fondant, strengthened
* 24 un-dipped cake pops on sticks (see pp242–43), 8 formed into cones with a flat base (for hats), and 8 with vertical ridges (for pumpkins)
* 400g (14oz) black candy melts
* 200g (7oz) orange candy melts
* edible felt-tip black pen
* 25g (scant 1oz) pink fondant

1 Colour a little yellow fondant with colouring paste, strengthen (see p87), and mould into 8 stalks. Roll out the black fondant, use the cutter to cut 8 circles, and then poke a central hole through each and place on scrunched foil. Allow all shapes to dry overnight.

2 Dip the hat (cone) and cat (round) cake pops into the melted black candy melts and set aside, upright, to harden. Dip the pumpkins into the melted orange melts and top with the stalks.

3 Roll out the remaining black fondant, and cut out the pumpkin features. Cut triangles for the cats' ears, and strips to wrap around the hats. Allow all to dry for 20 minutes. Use the yellow fondant and the pink fondant to create features for the cats, adding details to the cats' eyes with edible pen. Fix all of the cat and pumpkin features onto the pops with a little water.

4 Moisten the black circles, and slide them onto the hat cake-pop sticks. Moisten the black strips and fix to each hat.

Teddy bear mini cakes

These colourful cakes are layered with fondant and flower paste, and piped to create building blocks – perfect for a baby shower, newborn celebration, or an all-important first birthday. The shade of the coloured royal icing will deepen with time, so aim for one shade lighter.

 **TIMING** allow 1½ hours    **MAKES** 10

Equipment

* fondant roller
* square cutters: 7cm (2¾in), and 5cm (2in)
* fondant smoother
* mini bear cutter
* piping bag with tips (such as PME no. 1 and no. 5)

Ingredients

* 1.5kg (3lb 3oz) white fondant
* cornflour, for dusting
* 10 x 7cm (2¾in) square mini cakes, halved and filled with buttercream icing, crumb coated with ganache (see p29)
* 200g (7oz) each orange, lilac, blue, green, and pink fondant
* edible glue
* 200g (7oz) royal icing, for piping (see p35)
* black, orange, lilac, blue, green, and pink colouring pastes

1 Knead the white fondant until it is soft, and roll out a large circle on a cornflour-dusted surface, to 3mm (⅛in) thick. Cut the fondant into 12 squares to cover the cakes. Lay a square of fondant on each cake, and smooth it down over the sides with a fondant smoother. Trim off excess and leave to set for 30 minutes.

2 On a cornflour-dusted surface, roll out the orange fondant to 2mm (1⁄16in) thick. Cut out 10 squares with the large square cutter. Place the small cutter in the centre of each square and cut, leaving the outline. Allow to dry for 5 minutes, and then lift them onto baking parchment. Cut out 4 teddies and place alongside. Repeat with the lilac, blue, green, and pink fondant, so you have 10 square outlines and 4 teddies in each colour.

3 When the outlines are starting to firm, brush each with a little edible glue and press onto 5 sides of the cakes (leaving the base as it is). Press the edges together. Roll 20 tiny balls of white fondant with your hands, and press into circles. Moisten and fix to the faces of the teddies to make their snouts.

4 Colour a small amount of royal icing with black colouring paste. Fit a no. 1 tip to a piping bag and fill. Pipe details onto each of the teddies. Set aside to dry.

5 Divide the remaining royal icing between 5 bowls and tint each with colouring paste to match the fondant shades. Attach a no. 5 tip to a piping bag and fill with a shade of icing. Pipe a number or letter on 3 sides of each cake, piping the outline first and then filling in the inside.

6 Moisten the reverse of each teddy with a little water and fix to the remaining 2 sides of each cake, ensuring that the colours match.

Tip

If you are not confident at piping freehand, you can use letter and number cutters to emboss the surface of the squares and pipe to fill later on. Alternatively, cut them out from the appropriate fondant, and fix them in place with edible glue.

BRING IT ALL TOGETHER

Using cookie cutters see pp106-07

Basic royal icing piping see p75

Newborn celebration cake

This elegant cake is ideal for baby showers, newborn celebrations, and formal christenings. Tiny piped beads and dots highlight the fondant heart and ribbons, while swags, hearts, and buttons add beautiful, symmetrical detail. A template makes it easy to create perfect shapes.

 **TIMING** allow 1½ days, including drying time  **SERVES** 10

Equipment

* 28cm (11in) cake drum
* fondant roller
* multi-ribbon cutter, wavy edge
* stitching (quilting) tool
* set of circle cutters
* piping bag and tips (such as PME no. 1, 2, and 3)
* heart plunger cutters
* heart template (see p244)
* 1m (3ft) yellow ribbon
* craft glue

Ingredients

* 1kg (2¼lb) white fondant
* tylose powder
* icing sugar, for dusting
* 1kg (2¼lb) yellow fondant, strengthened (see p87)
* edible glue, diluted
* 20cm (8in) lemon sponge (see p229), filled with lemon buttercream icing
* 100g (3½oz) royal icing, for piping (see p35)

1 A day before you wish to serve, cover the cake drum with white fondant (see p51). Roll out the yellow fondant on an icing-sugar dusted surface to 5mm (¼in) thick, and cover the cake (see p50). Knead the remaining white fondant with tylose powder (see p87) and wrap both colours in cling film. Leave all to dry overnight.

2 Roll out the white fondant to 3mm (⅛in) thick. Using the multi-ribbon cutter, cut 16 wavy ribbons, 3 x 7.5cm (1¼ x 3in). Mark out 16 evenly spaced vertical lines around the side of the cake. Attach the ribbons to the marks with edible glue. Use the stitching tool to emboss vertical stitch marks on the ribbons.

3 Roll out a large piece of white fondant thinly and cut out eight 9 x 8cm/3½ x 3¼in rectangles. Create swags with 2 horizontal pleats, pinching the edges. Shape so that the swags neatly span 3 ribbons. Brush each end with a little water, and attach to the cake. Roll out more white fondant, and cut out 9 small circles using a cutter. Use a smaller cutter to emboss each "button". Use a no. 3 piping tip to cut out 2 holes in the centre of each. Fix to the cake where the swags join, reserving the extra button.

4 Roll out the yellow fondant and cut 8 small and 8 medium hearts, using plunger cutters. Fix to the cake. Roll out more white fondant, and cut around the heart template. Attach it to the top of the cake with diluted edible glue. Roll out the remaining yellow fondant, and cut out the baby feet. Stick on the fondant heart, and stitch around the edge with the stitching tool.

5 Fit the piping bag with a no. 1 tip. Pipe a line of royal icing picot dots around the heart. "Thread" each button. Pipe beads around the base of the cake, using a no. 2 tip. Fix the ribbon around the drum with craft glue, covering the join with a button.

BRING IT ALL TOGETHER

Using multi-ribbon cutters *see p118*

Modelling embellishments *see p96*

Piping dots, beads, and flowers *see p80*

Gingerbread house

With its intricate piping and fondant cut-out detail, this impressive gingerbread house is sure to please a crowd and provide a whimsical backdrop for your Christmas celebrations. Bake the gingerbread pieces in batches, and, once cool, use a serrated knife to refine the shapes.

 **TIMING** allow 2 days, including drying time

 **MAKES** 1 gingerbread house

Equipment

* rolling pin
* gingerbread house template (see p246)
* square, Christmas tree, heart, and circle cutters
* fondant smoother
* piping bag
* round tips (such as PME no. 1, 2, and 3)
* 28cm (11in) white fondant-covered square cake drum (see p51)
* 1m (3ft) red satin ribbon (1cm/½in wide)
* craft glue

Ingredients

* 1 batch gingerbread dough (see p235)
* 500g (1lb 2oz) royal icing, piping consistency (see p35)
* 100g (3½oz) red fondant, strengthened (see p87)
* cornflour, for dusting

1 Roll out the dough on a floured sheet of baking parchment, to about 5mm (¼in) thick. Using the template, cut out the pieces, including a spare panel (see Tips, opposite). Use cutters to cut out windows and trees.

2 Transfer the gingerbread and parchment to a baking tray. Bake in an oven preheated to 180°C (350°F/Gas 4), until golden. Cool in the tin and then move to a wire rack to cool.

3 Fit a piping bag with a no. 2 tip, and fill it with royal icing. Pipe tiles onto each roof panel, in a series of loops. Change to a no. 1 tip, and pipe patterns and picot dots (see p80) on the walls and the front of the house. Outline the windows and door, and pipe the surface of the chimney. Pipe an outline on the trees. Allow each piece to dry before assembling.

4 Assemble the house (see pp66–67). Assemble the chimney, then fix to the house. Use the spare panel to cut a 1cm (½in) wide strip, as long as the roof, to run along the top. Glue to the roof top with royal icing.

5 Roll out the red fondant on a cornflour-dusted surface and use cutters for tiny hearts, circles, and a wreath for the door. Roll small balls with your hands. Allow all to dry overnight. When dry, use a no. 1 tip to pipe royal icing onto the wreath in dots.

6 Switch to a no. 3 tip, and decorate the joins with piped beading (see p80). Fix the fondant shapes to the house with royal icing and allow it to harden for 24 hours. Once dry, lift the house and dot the underside of the walls with royal icing. Place on the covered drum, and pipe a snail trail at the base. Attach the ribbon around the drum (see Tips, opposite).

Tips

Bake an extra roof panel, which can be cut into the ridge line on the top of the roof and any extra supports. Glue the ribbon around the drum with craft glue, taking care to put the join at the back. Cover the join with a dot of royal icing.

BRING IT ALL TOGETHER

Making a template
see p57

Basic royal icing piping *see p75*

Building with ginger-bread *see pp66-67*

Using cookie cutters *see pp106-07*

Shades of pink

This spectacular shaded cake (also known as an ombré cake) is surprisingly easy to make. Gradated shades of pink sponge are sandwiched together with buttercream, and the cake is iced to match, with two pretty pink fondant butterflies resting on top.

 **TIMING** allow 1½ days, including drying time

 **SERVES** 20 finger portions; 10 for dessert

Equipment

* 5 x 15cm (6in) round cake tins, greased and lined (see p236)
* 15cm (6in) cake board
* turntable or lazy Susan
* scraper, smooth-edged
* butterfly plunger cutters in 2 sizes

Ingredients

* butter, for greasing
* 1½ batches of classic vanilla sponge batter (see p228)
* large tub of dark-pink (fuchsia) colouring paste
* 750g (1lb 10oz) buttercream icing (see p24)
* 25g (scant 1oz) dark-pink fondant, strengthened (see p87)

1 A day before you wish to serve, bake the cake. Preheat the oven to 180°C (350°F/Gas 4). Divide the sponge batter between 5 bowls. Add ⅛ teaspoon of pink colouring paste to the first bowl; ¼ teaspoon to the second; ½ teaspoon to the third; ¾ teaspoon to the fourth; and 1 teaspoon to the final bowl. Mix all bowls well until the batter is evenly coloured.

2 Pour the batter into the cake tins and bake for 20 minutes, test, and cool (see p238). Level the cakes (see p239). Spread a little buttercream icing onto the cake board, place the darkest cake on top, and move to the turntable.

3 Layer the cakes with buttercream icing (see p28), starting with the darkest at the bottom to the lightest at the top. Crumb coat the cake (see p29), and allow to rest for 1 hour.

4 Separate the remaining buttercream icing into 5 bowls and add the pink colouring paste to create 5 shades, from light to dark. Starting with the darkest shade of buttercream icing, ice the base up to about 2.5cm (1in). Continue up the cake using the remaining shades of buttercream icing, from dark to light, until the sides are covered. Ice the top with the lightest shade.

5 Pull the scraper across the side of the cake as you turn the turntable. Push a palette knife into the buttercream and spin the turntable, to create lines where the colour changes.

6 On a surface dusted with cornflour, roll out the dark-pink fondant to 2mm (¹⁄₁₆in) thick. Using a plunger cutter, cut out 2 butterflies and rest them in an open book, on a sheet of baking parchment. Dry overnight. Attach the butterflies to the top of the cake with a little buttercream icing.

BRING IT ALL TOGETHER

Filling a layer cake
see p28

Crumb coating a cake
see p29

Using plunger cutters
see pp101-03

Cupcake bouquet

Pipe a medley of cupcakes to create buttercream roses, and arrange them in a ceramic flowerpot to create a delightful centrepiece for any occasion. You could choose a larger pot to feed a crowd. While piping can take time to master, the end result is well worth the effort.

CUPCAKE BOUQUET **VARIATION:** HEART-SHAPED POSY CAKE *pp200-01*

 **TIMING** 1½ hrs    **MAKES** 12

Equipment

* large piping bag with injector tip, or plain round tip (see p74)
* large flower drop tip (such as Wilton no. 2D)
* polystyrene ball, about 10cm (4in) wide
* ceramic flowerpot, about 12.5cm (5in) wide
* decorative ribbon

Ingredients

* 12 cupcakes (see p240)
* 100g (3½oz) buttercream icing (see pp24–25)
* 100g (3½oz) buttercream icing, coloured pale pink
* 100g (3½oz) buttercream icing, coloured fuchsia
* 25g (scant 1oz) royal icing (see p34)

1 When the cupcakes have cooled, fill each cake with a little buttercream icing, using a plain round piping or injector tip attached to a large piping bag.

2 Fix a large flower drop tip to the same piping bag, and pipe a rose on 4 cupcakes. Start from the centre of the cupcake and swirl outwards in an anticlockwise direction, using even pressure, until the entire surface of the cupcake is covered with a piped rose.

3 Wash the piping bag or fit the same tip to a new piping bag, and fill the bag with pale pink buttercream icing. Pipe 4 more cupcakes, using the same technique. Pipe the remaining cupcakes with fuchsia buttercream icing, in the same way. Allow the cupcakes to set for 15 minutes.

4 Place the polystyrene ball into the flowerpot and press 6 cocktail sticks into the surface, about 9cm (3½in) apart. Spread a little royal icing on the base of a cupcake case, and press it firmly onto a cocktail stick that has been inserted into the ball. Hold in place for 30 seconds, until the icing begins to dry. Repeat for the next cupcake in the same colour, and then attach 2 cupcakes of each colour.

5 Wrap the flowerpot with decorative ribbon tied into a pretty bow. Place the remaining cupcakes around the flowerpot.

BRING IT ALL TOGETHER

Filling cupcakes
see p33

Piping a buttercream
rose *see p79*

BRING IT ALL TOGETHER

Covering a cake drum
see p51

Piping a buttercream
rose see p79

CUPCAKE BOUQUET **VARIATION**

Heart-shaped posy cake

Celebrate a special occasion, such as an anniversary or Valentine's day, with an elegant heart cake, extravagantly piped with lilac buttercream icing roses to create a flurry of flowers. For best results, start piping as soon as you've iced your cake, to ensure that your flowers adhere to the surface.

 **TIMING** allow 1½ days, including drying time

 **SERVES** 15

Equipment

* fondant roller
* 30cm (12in) heart-shaped cake drum
* fondant smoother
* piping bag
* large drop flower tip (such as Wilton no. 2D)
* 1m (3ft) light green satin ribbon (1cm/½in wide)
* craft glue

Ingredients

* cornflour, for dusting
* 250g (9oz) white fondant, strengthened (see p87)
* 20cm (8in) 2-layer heart-shaped vanilla sponge cake, filled and crumb coated with buttercream icing (see p29)
* 500g (1lb 2oz) buttercream icing (pp24–25), coloured with lilac colouring paste

1 A day before you wish to serve the cake, on a flat surface dusted with cornflour, roll out the strengthened white fondant to 2mm (¹⁄₁₆in) thick and cover the heart-shaped cake drum using a fondant smoother. Set aside to dry overnight.

2 Place the crumb-coated cake on a flat surface and fill a piping bag, fitted with a large drop flower tip, with lilac-coloured buttercream icing.

3 Starting on the top of the cake, pipe a series of roses with the buttercream icing, starting from the middle of a rose and applying even pressure as you pipe in an anticlockwise direction. Each rose should measure about 2cm (¾in) in diameter.

4 Continue across the entire surface of the cake and the sides, until you have covered it completely. Fill any spaces between the roses with small piped buttercream stars.

5 Using a large, wide spatula, lift the cake onto the covered cake drum. Fix the ribbon around the base of the cake drum with craft glue, taking care to ensure that the join is at the back.

Handbag cake

This whimsical designer bag cake, with its quilted flap and metallic chain, is incredibly realistic and easier to make than it looks. Use a veining tool to create authentic detail on the sides and main body.

 **TIMING** allow 1½ days, including drying time

 **SERVES** 40 finger portions

Equipment

* fondant roller
* fondant smoother
* veining tool
* 33cm (13in) fondant-covered cake drum
* 20cm (8in) round cake board or tin, to use as a template
* stitching (quilting) tool
* wide round piping tip (such as PME no. 4)
* 1m (3ft) white satin ribbon (1cm/½in wide)
* craft glue

1 Halve the square sponge cake across the centre, and spread the top of one half with buttercream icing. Stack the other on top. Freeze for 2 hours. Carve into a wedge shape and crumb coat (see p29). Allow to set for 1 hour.

2 On a surface dusted with cornflour, roll out the lilac fondant to about 4mm (⅙in) thick. Cover the cake, smoothing the fondant with the fondant smoother. Cut off the excess, and tuck the edges under the cake. Move the cake to the covered cake drum. Smooth with the fondant smoother before adding detail. Add shallow creases to the bag with the veining tool.

3 Cut a square with a rounded edge from more lilac fondant, to form the flap for the bag. To create the semi-circle shape, cut around the edge of the round cake board. For the quilting pattern, quilt with the stitching tool at 2.5cm (1in) intervals. Moisten the back of the flap with a little water and fix to the front of the cake.

4 To make the handles, roll out the black flower paste on a flat surface dusted with cornflour and cut 2 strips measuring 20cm (8in) by 3.5cm (1⅓in). Stitch around the edges of each strip with the stitching tool.

BRING IT ALL TOGETHER

 →  →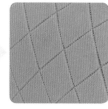

Carving and covering cakes *see p65*

Modelling embellishments *see pp96–97*

Quilting *see p156*

Ingredients

* 23cm (9in) 2-layer square vanilla sponge cake (see p228), levelled and filled with buttercream (see p28)
* 100g (3½oz) buttercream icing (see p24)
* cornflour, for dusting
* 1.5kg (3lb 3oz) lilac fondant
* 50g (1¾oz) black flower paste
* 50g (1¾oz) black fondant, strengthened (see p87)
* 50g (1¾oz) grey flower paste
* edible silver lustre dust
* rejuvenator spirit or vodka
* 25g (scant 1oz) royal icing
* edible glue

Tip

To make a charm, model a bow from black fondant. Make a thin rope with the grey fondant and join it around the handles. Make a single half-link and fix it to the top of the bow. Paint the chain with lustre dust mixed with rejuvenator spirit.

5 Turn the strips over and moisten the backs with water. Fold and then press together the strips, leaving 5cm (2in) flat at each end. Arrange in a semi-circle and allow to dry overnight.

6 To make the black trim, roll a thin rope of black strengthened fondant with your hands, making it as long as you can. Run the fondant smoother over the rope to make it smooth and even. Work on one section at a time, making sure the rope is long enough to trim the section of the bag you are working on. Brush a little water around the edge of the bag and the flap, and fix the black rope to it.

7 Roll out another thin rope of grey flower paste, and cut it into about 15 pieces, each about 7cm (2¾in) in length. Wet one end and join together to form a link, smoothing the join between your thumb and forefinger. Link with the next piece of fondant rope, repeating until you have a chain long enough to run down one side of the cake and spill out onto the board.

8 Fix the chain to one side of the handbag with a little water, starting from the top and carefully working downwards. Repeat on the other side of the cake, making a chain of the same length and fixing it to the cake.

9 To join the lengths of chains on the board, roll out a black fondant shoulder strap (about 10 x 3cm/4 x 1½in). Stitch each side with the stitching tool. Use a piping tip (PME no. 4) to cut out 2 circles for the chains to go through. Create another link for both of the chains, and thread them through the hole on each side of the strap. Mix the silver lustre dust with rejuvenator spirit and paint the chains. If you get paint on the cake, dip a muslin cloth in rejuvenator spirit and dab it off.

10 When the handles are dry, fix them onto the cake with a little royal icing. Pop a support under the handles to keep them upright while the royal icing dries.

11 Use the end of the piping tip (PME no. 4) to cut 4 circles from the black fondant. Fix them to the handles with a little water. Paint with the silver lustre dust mixed with some rejuvenator spirit. Glue the ribbon around the covered drum, taking care to place the join at the back of the drum. Dot the join with royal icing.

Handbag cake pp202–03

Blossom stencil cake pp206–07

Blossom stencil cake

This delightful two-tiered sponge cake is wrapped in white fondant and adorned with pretty fondant blossoms. A simple pattern of stripes is stencilled around the bottom tier in fuchsia royal icing.

TIMING allow 2 days, including drying time  **SERVES** 20

Equipment

* 2 x round cake boards: 17cm (6¾in) and 12.5cm (5in) in diameter
* fondant roller
* striped stencil
* masking tape
* 4 dowels
* multi-ribbon cutter, straight edges
* small blossom plunger cutter
* flower mat or foam
* ball tool
* piping bag
* small piping tip (such as PME no. 0 or no. 1)

1 Two days before you wish to serve, place each cake on its board and crumb coat them with a thin layer of buttercream icing (see p29). Allow to set overnight.

2 Roll out a sheet of white fondant on a surface dusted with icing sugar and cover the largest cake and board. Smooth carefully and repeat with the smaller cake and board. Set aside. Allow the cakes to set for 1–2 days.

3 Scoop up any excess white fondant and strengthen with tylose powder (see p87). Rest, covered with cling film, for 24 hours until it is pliable.

4 When the fondant on the larger cake is dry, stencil the cake. Use a ruler to mark about 1cm (½in) down from the top of the cake, and prick the surface of the cake lightly at this point, all around, as a guide for the stencil.

5 Working around the cake, hold the stencil against the surface and apply masking tape to hold it in place. Smooth over the pink royal icing with a palette knife, working in one direction. Allow each section to dry a little before moving the

BRING IT ALL TOGETHER

Stencilling the sides of a cake see p125

Building tiered cakes see p68

Using multi-ribbon cutters see p118

Using edible dusts see p136

Ingredients

* 17cm (6¾in) round vanilla sponge cake (3 x 2.5cm/1in levelled layers, sandwiched with buttercream icing, see p28)
* 12.5cm (5in) round vanilla sponge cake (2 x 2.5cm/1in levelled layers, sandwiched with buttercream icing, see p28)
* 200g (7oz) buttercream icing (see p24)
* 1kg (2¼lb) white fondant
* icing sugar, for dusting
* tylose powder
* cornflour, for dusting
* 100g (3½oz) pink royal icing (see pp34–35)
* 100g (3½oz) pink fondant, strengthened (see p87)
* orange petal dust
* pink petal dust
* 50g (1¾oz) white royal icing, for piping (see p35)
* fresh flowers, preferably edible, to decorate

stencil and stencilling again. Continue until the whole circumference is stencilled. Touch up any uneven areas with a paintbrush dipped in a little water.

6 Insert the dowels, cut to size, into the larger cake (see p68), and place the smaller cake and board on top, taking care to centre it. Secure with royal or buttercream icing.

7 Dust a surface with a little cornflour, and roll out the pink fondant to about 5mm (¼in) thick. Use the ribbon cutter to cut a ribbon the same length as the circumference of the cake, plus a few millimetres (about ¹⁄₁₆in) more. It should be about 50cm (20in) long and 3cm (1¼in) wide.

8 Dip a paintbrush in a little water and moisten a line around the base of the smaller cake, about 3cm (1¼in) up the cake. Wrap the ribbon where the cake has been moistened, by rolling it up and carefully unrolling it as you apply it to the cake.

9 Roll out the strengthened white fondant (from step 3) on a dusted surface to about 2mm (¹⁄₁₆in) thick. Lightly dust the surface of the fondant with cornflour and use a small blossom plunger cutter to cut out about 25 blossoms.

10 Place the blossoms on the flower mat and use a ball tool to soften and thin the edges, curling the petals. Leave them to dry for about 10 minutes.

11 Brush half of the blossoms with orange petal dust and the other half with pink petal dust. Attach a small tip (such as a PME no. 0 or no. 1) to the piping bag and fill it with white royal icing. Pipe little beads or dots into the centre of each blossom (see p80). Attach the tumbling blossoms to the cake with a little more royal icing.

12 For a final vibrant touch, decorate the top tier with bright fresh flowers to complement the colours of the blossoms.

Suitcase cake

Say "Bon voyage" or celebrate a special holiday with this suitcase, complete with hand-stitched trim, metallic painted fastenings, and, if desired, edible travel stickers printed with images of your favourite holiday destinations.

 **TIMING** allow 1½ days, including drying time  **SERVES** 40

Equipment

* fondant roller
* cutting wheel
* 28cm (11in) rectangular fondant-covered drum
* multi-ribbon cutter
* stitching (quilting) tool
* small round piping tip
* circle cutters: 2cm (¾in), and 1.5cm (⅔in)

Ingredients

* cornflour, for dusting
* 2.5kg (5½lb) brown fondant
* 2 x sponge cakes 18 x 28cm (7 x 11in) sandwiched and crumb coated with buttercream (see p29)
* 200g (7oz) lilac fondant, strengthened (see p87)
* 50g (1¾oz) each of yellow and dark brown fondant, strengthened (see p87)
* edible gold lustre dust, mixed into paint (see p136)

1 On a cornflour-dusted surface, roll out the brown fondant to a large rectangle that is 3mm (⅛in) thick. Cover the cake with the fondant (see p50). Mark a line halfway up the cake (about 5cm/2in) from the base, and use a cutting wheel to emboss a horizontal line. Transfer the cake to the covered cake board, so it sits towards the back. Leave the cake to set overnight.

2 Roll out the lilac fondant to 2mm (¹⁄₁₆in) thick on a cornflour-dusted surface. Use a ribbon cutter to cut two 1cm (½in) strips to run around the top and bottom edges of the cake. Fix to the cake around the base and on the top edge. Place the join at the back. Use the stitching tool to detail both edges of the strips.

3 Roll out the strengthened yellow fondant, and cut out 2 rectangles (4 x 2.5cm/1½ x 1in). Trim off the corners and use the piping tip to emboss 4 holes on each. Apply to the bottom half of the cake with a little water, 3cm (1¼in) in from each side. Cut 2 smaller yellow rectangles, about 3 x 1cm (1¼ x ½in) in size. Shape and emboss as above, and fix to the top half of the cake. Roll out 2 more rectangles, about 1.5 x 1cm (⅔ x ½in) in size, and fix to the bottom half, 4cm (1½in) apart.

4 Cut out 2 circles using the large cutter, and 2 more using the small cutter. Moisten the backs with a little water and fix the large circles on the bottom plates and the small on top of these. Model 2 catches and fix with water to the top and bottom plates. Paint all of the yellow fixings with the gold lustre dust paint.

5 Roll a sausage of strengthened dark brown fondant (1.5 x 15cm/⅔ x 6in), to create a handle. Flatten and mark with the stitching tool. Fix to the suitcase, holding it in place for a few minutes so that it sticks. Attach images, if desired (see Tip).

Tip

Print images that are about 7cm (2¾in) in size on edible icing sheets (see pp150–51). Peel off the backing paper and fix them to a sheet of white flower paste rolled to 3mm (⅛in) thick. Allow to dry. Cut out with a scalpel and fix to the suitcase with water.

BRING IT ALL TOGETHER

Using multi-ribbon cutters *see p118*

Using edible dusts *see p136*

Using icing sheets *see pp150–51*

Cigarillo wedding cake

This spectacular wedding cake is topped with modelled chocolate roses, wrapped in dark chocolate cigarillos, and embellished with chocolate ribbons. Polystyrene separates the layers to add height and allows you to tuck the roses neatly into the spaces below each tier.

CIGARILLO WEDDING CAKE **VARIATION:** WEDDING MINI CAKES *p213*

 **TIMING** allow 1½ days, including drying time

 **SERVES** 120 finger portions; 60 for dessert

Equipment

* fondant roller
* 33cm (13in) round cake drum
* 2 x polystyrene separators: 12.5 x 4cm (5 x 1½in) and 18 x 4cm (7 x 1½in)
* rose petal cutters
* 9 dowels
* 2 x round cake boards: 15cm (6in) and 20cm (8in)
* multi-ribbon cutters, straight sides

1 A day before you wish to serve the cake, on a flat surface dusted with icing sugar, roll out a ball of dark chocolate fondant, strengthen with tylose powder (see p87), and cover the cake drum (see p51). Cover the 2 polystyrene cake separators with the same fondant. Allow to dry overnight.

2 On the same day, model the roses using strengthened dark chocolate fondant. Make 55 medium chocolate roses, each about 6cm (2¼in) in diameter with about 12–15 petals (see p88). Use the petal cutter to help. Allow to harden for about 1 day. If you are making your own, prepare your cigarillos (see p43), and allow to harden for at least 24 hours.

3 Place the largest iced cake on the covered cake drum, fixing it with a little melted chocolate. Insert 5 dowels, cut to the height of the cake. Place the middle tier on its corresponding board, and insert 4 dowels, cut to the height of the cake. Place the top tier on its board and set aside.

METHOD CONTINUES · · · ·

BRING IT ALL TOGETHER

Modelling a fondant rose *see p88*

Building tiered cakes *see p68*

Using multi-ribbon cutters *see p118*

Modelling embellishments *see p96*

Tips

If desired, very gently steam the cake using an iron, about 10cm (4in) from the surface, or lightly spray with glaze (see p159). Do not handle the cigarillos too much, as they will become dull. Wear a pair of cotton gloves, to help.

Ingredients

* icing sugar, for dusting
* 3kg (6½lb) dark chocolate fondant
* tylose powder
* 1.4kg (3lb) dark chocolate cigarillos (see p43)
* 200g (7oz) dark chocolate, melted, for securing cakes
* 3 x chocolate sponge cakes (see p232): 10cm (4in), 15cm (6in), and 20cm (8in) in diameter, with three 2.5cm (1in) layers each; levelled, sandwiched, and iced with chocolate buttercream icing (see p25, you will need about 750g/1lb 10oz in total)
* 100g (3½oz) white chocolate modelling clay (see pp44–45)

4 Fix the chocolate cigarillos around the sides of each cake by gently pushing them into the buttercream icing. Use more buttercream icing, if required. Leave to dry for 30 minutes.

5 When the cigarillos are firmly attached to the cake, place the largest covered separator directly on top of the bottom tier, fixing it into place with melted chocolate. Place the middle tier on top of the separator, and fix it into place with melted chocolate.

6 Place the smaller separator on top of the middle tier of the cake, and fix with melted chocolate. This should be topped with the top tier of the cake, again fixed with chocolate.

7 Measure the circumference of the bottom tier (about 81cm/32in). On a surface dusted with icing sugar, roll out the strengthened dark chocolate fondant to about 3mm (⅛in) thick. Prepare the ribbon cutter with straight sides and cut a ribbon with a width of 3cm (1¼in). It needs to be just a little longer than the circumference of the cake. Set aside, taking care to keep it flat.

8 Repeat for the middle and top tiers of the cakes, measuring each circumference and cutting a 3cm (1¼in) wide ribbon to the appropriate length. You should have 3 ribbons in all.

9 Roll out the white chocolate modelling clay on a surface dusted with icing sugar, to 3mm (⅛in) thick. Cut 3 ribbons the same length as the dark chocolate ones, but only 1cm (½in) wide. Lay the white chocolate ribbons on top of the dark chocolate ribbons of the same size, taking care to align them in the centre of each. Gently rub to adhere.

10 Brush melted chocolate around the base of each cake tier and fix the ribbons in place over the chocolate.

11 On a surface dusted with icing sugar, roll out another length of strengthened chocolate fondant to 3mm (⅛in). Use the ribbon cutter to create six 10cm (4in) lengths of ribbon, each 3cm (1¼in) wide. Form into bows, using extra fondant to create the centre. Fix to the join of the ribbon on each tier with chocolate. Decorate the top of the cake with the roses, using chocolate to adhere, and fill the spaces between the tiers with the chocolate roses.

CIGARILLO WEDDING CAKE **VARIATION**

Wedding mini cakes

Iced with ganache, wrapped in chocolate fondant and finished off with a pretty ribbon and chocolate roses, these gorgeous miniature wedding cakes make an ideal favour or sophisticated dessert. For completely edible cakes, cut your ribbons from white-chocolate modelling clay instead (see opposite).

 **TIMING** allow 1½ days, including drying time

SERVES 12

Equipment

* fondant roller
* small rose leaf plunger cutter
* scraper, smooth-edged
* fondant smoother
* 2.5m (8ft) ivory grosgrain ribbon, 12mm (½in) wide

Ingredients

* 1.2kg (2¾lb) dark chocolate fondant
* tylose powder
* 12 x 7cm (2¾in) mini round chocolate sponge cakes, halved and filled with chocolate buttercream icing (see p25)
* 900g (2lb) dark chocolate ganache (see p38)
* icing sugar, for dusting
* 50g (1¾oz) dark chocolate, melted
* edible glue

1 Strengthen 200g (7oz) of the dark chocolate fondant with tylose powder (see p87) and allow to rest overnight. When the fondant is pliable, hand-model 12 small roses, 2.5cm (1in) wide. Set aside to dry for about 30 minutes. Roll out more strengthened fondant to 2mm (¹⁄₁₆in) thick and use the rose leaf plunger cutter to cut out 24 leaves. Curve the tips, and leave to dry for about 30 minutes. Use a palette knife to spread the sides and top of each cake with ganache. Run the icing scraper over the surface.

2 On a surface dusted with icing sugar, roll out the remaining dark chocolate fondant to 3mm (⅛in) thick. Cut out 12 circles that are large enough to cover each cake, and smooth the fondant down over the cakes with a fondant smoother. Trim off any excess from the base, and allow to rest for 30 minutes.

3 Use the melted chocolate to fix a rose and 2 leaves to the top of each cake. Cut the ribbon into 12 equal lengths, and wrap around the base of each cake, fixing the join with edible glue.

Filigree wedding cake

Beautifully piped with filigree lace and adorned with fondant roses, leaves, and appliqué blossoms, this exquisite, three-tiered cake is perfect for a wedding. Dress the cake with fresh edible flowers instead, if you desire.

FILIGREE WEDDING CAKE **VARIATION:** BRIDAL LACE CUPCAKES *p217*

TIMING allow 4 days, including drying time

SERVES 90-100 finger portions

Equipment

* 3 x cake boards: 10cm (4in), 20cm (8in), and 25cm (10in) in diameter
* fondant roller
* 18-gauge florist's wire
* calyx cutter
* set of leaf plunger cutters
* ball tool
* rose leaf veiner
* template (see p245)
* masking tape
* scribing tool
* turntable or lazy Susan
* small piping bags with tips (such as PME no. 1 and 3)

1 Four days before you wish to serve the cake, place the fruitcakes on their boards, and brush with apricot glaze. Dust a flat surface with icing sugar, and roll out the marzipan. Cover the cakes (see p37) and allow to dry overnight.

2 When the marzipan is dry, brush it with a little water. Roll out the white fondant to 4mm (⅙in) thick on a surface dusted with icing sugar, and use to cover the cakes (see p50). Trim off the excess and allow the cakes to rest for 2–3 days. Cover the remaining fondant with cling film, and set aside.

3 Make sugar roses (see p88) by forming 6–7 cones of fuchsia flower paste on 18-gauge florist's wire. Place upright to dry for several days (see p112). When the cones are dry, grease a surface with white vegetable fat and roll out the flower paste to 1mm (¹⁄₁₆in) thick. Model open roses over 5 of the dried cones. On the remaining cones, create rose buds with 5 petals. Roll a small ball of leaf-green flower paste, and thread it onto the wire so that each cone has a base. Roll out more leaf-green fondant and then use the calyx cutter to cut calyxes. Slip them onto the base of

METHOD CONTINUES · · · ·

BRING IT ALL TOGETHER

Covering a cake with marzipan *see p37*

Modelling a fondant rose *see p88*

Piping filigree with royal icing *see p81*

Building tiered cakes *see p68*

Tips

You could fix the roses onto
a greased cocktail stick to dry,
instead of wire. Lift off the dry
roses and fix them onto the cake
(step 10). Fix wired flower paste
roses to the cake by pressing the
wires into plastic flower
picks (see p18).

- ✻ small embossed blossom
  plunger cutter
- ✻ 33cm (13in) fondant-
  covered round cake drum
  (see p51)
- ✻ 11 dowels
- ✻ 1m (3ft) white satin
  ribbon (1cm/½in wide)
- ✻ craft glue

Ingredients

- ✻ 3 x fruitcakes (p233):
  15cm (6in), 20cm (8in)
  and 25cm (10in) in
  diameter, each 7.5cm
  (3in) deep
- ✻ 300ml (10fl oz) apricot
  glaze (see p37)
- ✻ icing sugar, for dusting
- ✻ 2kg (4½lb) marzipan
- ✻ 3kg (6½lb) white fondant
- ✻ 200g (7oz) fuchsia
  flower paste
- ✻ white vegetable fat,
  for greasing
- ✻ 100g (3½oz) leaf-green
  flower paste
- ✻ edible petal dust in deep
  burgundy and pink
- ✻ 500g (1lb) royal icing,
  for piping (see p35)
- ✻ cornflour, for dusting
- ✻ edible pearl lustre dust
- ✻ rejuvenator spirit
  or vodka

the roses, pushing the wire through the centre. Moisten and press onto the green ball at the base of the rose. Place on the stand to dry overnight. Once dry, dust the petal edges with a dark shade of petal dust, and steam (see p143). Allow to dry, and then carefully remove the wires, or insert into flower picks (see Tips, p215).

4 Roll out the green flower paste to 1mm (¹⁄₁₆in) thick, cut the leaves using the rose leaf veiner, and soften the edges with a ball tool. Dry overnight. Dust the edges with pink petal dust and steam. Allow to dry.

5 When the cakes are set, cut out scalloped-edge templates for all 3 tiers. Attach them around the tiers and hold in place with masking tape. Using a scribing tool, mark along the edge. Remove the templates and place the first cake on the turntable. Fill a piping bag with royal icing and attach a no. 1 tip. Outline the lace pattern by piping a scalloped line around the edge of the scribed template mark. Repeat for each cake.

6 On a cornflour-dusted surface, roll out the remaining white fondant to 1mm (¹⁄₁₆in) thick, and cut out about 18 blossoms using the plunger cutter. Fix to the scalloped sections with water.

7 When all the blossoms are applied, pipe the filigree infill in the remaining space. Repeat for each tier, and then pipe tiny, evenly spaced picot dots above the scallop outline on each cake.

8 Dowel the cakes, using 6 dowels for the bottom tier and 5 dowels for the top. Place the bottom tier, on its board, onto the covered cake drum, using royal icing to secure, and then stack the tiers on top (see p68), securing each with royal icing.

9 Fill a piping bag with royal icing, and pipe a snail's trail (see p80) around the base of each cake, using a no. 3 tip. Paint it with pearl lustre dust mixed with rejuvenator spirit.

10 Use royal icing to fix the roses onto the cake, or, if still wired, press in the flower picks (see Tips, p215). Cut a length of ribbon to fit around the base of the covered cake drum, and fix with double-sided tape or craft glue. Cover the join with a series of piped picot dots.

FILIGREE WEDDING CAKE **VARIATION**

Bridal lace cupcakes

These cupcakes have royal icing filigree and a piped snail's trail painted with pearl lustre dust. Ideal as wedding favours or a sweet treat to accompany a cake, they provide the perfect finishing touch for a special day. Measure the surface of your cupcakes first, to ensure that the fondant circles will cover the top exactly.

 **TIMING** 2 hrs    **MAKES** 12

Equipment

* fondant roller
* circle cutter, about 7.5cm (3in) in diameter
* small piping bag
* fine piping tips (such as PME no. 1 and 2)

Ingredients

* icing sugar, for dusting
* 200g (7oz) white fondant
* 12 cupcakes (see p240), lightly iced with buttercream icing (see pp24–25)
* 150g (5½oz) royal icing, for piping (see p35)
* edible pearl lustre dust
* rejuvenator spirit or vodka
* 12 edible diamonds

1 On a surface dusted with icing sugar, roll out the white fondant to about 3mm (⅛in) thick and use the cutter to cut out 12 circles. Moisten the backs of the circles with a little water and place them on top of the cupcakes, smoothing them until flat.

2 Fit a no. 1 tip to a small piping bag and fill with royal icing. Pipe the surface of each cupcake with delicate filigree (see p81). Leave a border of about 2mm (¹⁄₁₆in) around the outside of each fondant circle.

3 Fit a no. 2 tip to the piping bag and pipe delicate beading around the outside of the fondant circle (see p80). Allow to dry for 1 hour, or until hard.

4 Mix together some edible pearl lustre dust with rejuvenator spirit, and carefully paint the piped border. Place a dot of royal icing in the centre of each cupcake and place an edible diamond on top.

Festive yule log

This rich, indulgent, and gloriously authentic Christmas yule log, complete with glistening snowflakes, is the perfect centrepiece for all winter celebrations. Rich chocolate buttercream icing and marbled brown and white fondant create a feast for the eyes and the taste buds.

 **TIMING** allow 1½ days, including drying time    **SERVES** 10

Equipment

* snowflake plunger cutters
* 20 x 28cm (8 x 11in) Swiss roll tin, lined with baking parchment

Ingredients

* 50g (1¾oz) white fondant, strengthened (see p87) and rolled out to 3mm (⅛in) thick
* 4 eggs
* 100g (3½oz) caster sugar
* 100g (3½oz) plain flour
* 3 tbsp cocoa powder
* ½ tsp baking powder
* 200ml (7fl oz) double cream
* 1 tsp vanilla extract
* 600g (1lb 5oz) chocolate buttercream icing
* 50g (1¾oz) each of 3 shades of brown fondant
* cornflour, for dusting
* edible glitter
* icing sugar, for dusting

1 Make the snowflakes a day ahead of serving the log. Cut them out from the white fondant with the snowflake plunger cutters. Set aside on baking parchment to dry overnight.

2 Preheat the oven to 180°C (350°F/Gas 4). In a large bowl, whisk together the eggs, sugar, and 1 tbsp of water. Beat for 5 minutes, until fluffy. Sift the flour, cocoa, and baking powder into the bowl, and fold into the egg mixture. Pour the mixture into the Swiss roll tin and bake for 12 minutes, until springy to the touch. Meanwhile, using an electric whisk, whisk together the cream and vanilla extract on a high setting until you get soft peaks. Set aside.

3 Turn out the cake onto a sheet of baking parchment, on a flat surface. Peel the paper from the back of the cake while still hot and then roll up the cake lengthways into a tight roll, with the paper inside. Turn the log so that it sits on the seam, and cool.

4 Uncurl the log, remove the parchment, and spread with the whipped cream. Re-roll the cake and place on a plate with the seam side down. Allow to set for 1 hour. Create a branch by cutting a quarter of the log off, at an angle, and placing it at the side. Gently warm the chocolate buttercream icing to spreadable consistency, and use a palette knife to cover the log. Use a fork to score patterns into the surface.

5 Form sausages with each shade of brown fondant and then twist them together. Roll the twist out onto a surface dusted with cornflour and fold and roll again until it is striped. Roll into a log and roll flat again, creating a spiral pattern. Cut out 3 circles, and fix to the ends of the log and branch with buttercream. Dab the surface of the snowflakes with water and scatter with edible glitter. Use them to decorate the log, dusting it with icing sugar.

Tip

Place the snowflakes on kitchen paper before sprinkling with glitter. You can then collect any excess and tip it back into the container. You can paint the surface of the snowflakes with edible pearl lustre dust mixed with rejuvenator spirit.

BRING IT ALL TOGETHER

Using plunger cutters
see pp101-03

Working with edible glitter see p153

Festive fruitcake

This simple yet elegant Christmas cake is covered in smooth royal icing and topped with a delicate robin runout. Piped icicles decorate the top and a pretty fondant bow encircles the fruitcake, which can be made weeks in advance of your special celebration.

FESTIVE FRUITCAKE **VARIATION:** CHRISTMAS CAKE POPS *p223*

 **TIMING** allow 4 days, including drying time

 **SERVES** 20

Equipment

* fondant roller
* robin runout templates (see p244)
* masking tape
* food-grade acetate sheets
* 4 piping bags
* fine piping tips (such as PME no. 1 and 2)
* turntable or lazy Susan
* cranked palette knife
* 30cm (12in) round cake drum, royal-iced
* multi-ribbon cutter, straight sides
* 1m (3ft) white satin ribbon (1cm/½in wide)
* craft glue

Ingredients

* icing sugar, for dusting
* 1 quantity marzipan (see p36)

1 Four days before you wish to serve the cake, roll out the marzipan to 7.5mm (¼in thick) on an icing-sugar dusted surface. Brush the surface of the cake with apricot glaze, and cover with marzipan (see p37). Set aside to dry for 2–3 days. Trace the robin template on a sheet of paper. Use masking tape to secure it to a flat surface. Cover with acetate and secure with masking tape. Lightly grease the surface with white vegetable fat.

2 Place half of the piping-consistency royal icing in a bowl, double-wrap with cling film, and set aside. Divide the remainder into 4 small pots. Use colouring paste to achieve the different colours for the robin.

3 Fit a small tip (no. 1) to each piping bag, and fill each with a different colour. Using the right colour for each part of the robin (e.g., yellow for the beak), pipe the outline of each part of the robin. Make sure that all the lines touch each other, as shown on p140. Keep the piping bags upright with a wet sponge around the tip, to prevent them from drying out. Make a second outline for the robin's wing on a separate sheet of acetate. Leave to dry hard for a few hours. Decant each piping bag into its own bowl and cover tightly with cling film. Set aside.

4 When the outlines are hard, thin the coloured icings, one by one, with some water, adding a drop at a time until it reaches the right consistency. Transfer each icing batch to a piping bag fitted with a slightly bigger tip (no. 2), and begin your runouts (see p140). Allow each section to dry for about

METHOD CONTINUES ᐧ ᐧ ᐧ ᐧ

BRING IT ALL TOGETHER

Piping royal icing runouts *see pp140-41*

Piping dots, beads, and flowers *see p80*

Using edible dusts *see p136*

Modelling embellishments *see p96*

* 20cm (8in) fruitcake (see p233)
* 90ml (3fl oz) apricot glaze
* white vegetable fat, for greasing
* 150g (5½oz) royal icing, for piping (see p35)
* red, brown, yellow, and black colouring pastes
* 1 quantity royal icing (see p34)
* edible pearl lustre dust
* cornflour, for dusting
* 200g (7oz) red fondant, strengthened (see p87)

Tip

To create bauble mini cakes, form 5cm (2in) cake-pop balls (see p242), and brush with jam. Wrap 125g (4½oz) of fondant around each ball, smoothing, cutting off excess, and then rolling in your hands. Cover with festive fondant decorations.

10 minutes before moving on to another colour. Fill in the second robin's wing in the same way. To achieve a good shine, allow to dry in a warm, dry place for several days.

5 While the robin runout is drying, place the cake on a turntable. Apply a layer of royal icing (not piping consistency) to the marzipan with the cranked palette knife, covering the sides first. Allow to dry, and then apply another coat. Dry and add another layer of icing until the sides are lovely and smooth.

6 When the sides are dry, ice the top, following the same steps. Try to get a sharp edge where the sides meet the top. Allow to dry. Place the cake on the royal-iced cake drum, taking care to centre it. Fill 2 piping bags with piping consistency royal icing and attach a no. 1 tip to one bag and a no. 2 tip to the other. Pipe a row of dots onto the surface of the cake, where the top meets the sides. Create icicles by piping dots that become a little smaller as you work down the cake in vertical lines. Make the lines uneven in length, to provide a more realistic effect. When dry, dust with pearl lustre dust (see p136).

7 Dust a flat surface with cornflour, and roll out the red fondant to 2mm (1/16in) thick. Use the ribbon cutter to cut a ribbon long enough to wrap around the base of the cake, 2cm (¾in) wide. Moisten the back and wrap around the cake with the join at the front. Roll out another length of red fondant, and create a bow (see p96). Moisten the back and apply to the cake at the join.

8 Very carefully lift the dry robin runout from the acetate sheet, using a thin metal palette knife. You may have to move the knife gently from side to side to release it. Affix to the centre of the cake with a small dot of royal icing. Dot a little royal icing onto the robin's wing portion of the runout, and then carefully lift the second robin's wing on top, guiding it into place with your fingers. Allow to dry for about an hour.

9 Glue the satin ribbon around the base of the iced cake drum, using craft glue. Pipe a few icicle dots over the join at the back of the cake.

FESTIVE FRUITCAKE **VARIATION**

Christmas cake pops

Guaranteed to bring a smile, these delightful Christmas cake pops are a lovely way to offer a sweet treat or party favour with minimum fuss. Use dabbed water to fix on your fondant decorations. To finish, you can wrap a length of ribbon around the stick of each cake pop.

 **TIMING** allow ½ day, including drying time

 **MAKES** 16 (8 of each design)

Equipment

* 16 cake-pop sticks
* fondant roller
* small piping bag with fine tip (such as PME no. 1)

Ingredients

* 50g (1¾oz) brown flower paste
* 25g (1oz) each brown, black orange, and white fondant, strengthened (see p87)
* 16 un-dipped cake pops, stick inserted (see p242)
* 400g (14oz) white chocolate melts
* 200g (7oz) milk chocolate melts
* 100g (3½oz) red fondant, strengthened (see p87)
* 50g (1¾oz) royal icing, for piping (see p35)
* edible white petal dust
* edible pink petal dust
* 50g (1¾oz) green fondant
* edible black pen

1 Make 16 antlers with pea-sized balls of brown flower paste. Roll into 4cm (1½in) sticks with pointed ends. Knead the orange fondant into 8 carrots, shaping peppercorn-size pieces into cones and scoring the surface. Allow the shapes to dry.

2 When dry, dip half the cake pops in melted white chocolate melts and press the carrot noses into the surface while soft. Dip the rest in the melted milk chocolate melts and press the antlers into the surface. Set the pops upright, to harden.

3 Use the brown and red fondant to decorate the reindeer. Score the smile with a piping tip, and use white and black fondant for the eyes, adding a piped royal icing gleam.

4 Dust the snowmen with edible white petal dust and a little edible pink petal dust for the cheeks. Use red and green fondant to model hats and the holly. Roll tiny balls of black fondant for the eyes. Create a smile with the edible black pen.

Ruffled cake

This elegant celebration cake is decorated with rows of fondant ruffles in ascending shades of blue, and topped with a wrapped fondant rose. Before you decorate the cake, cover the cake drum with fondant that has been strengthened with tylose powder (see p51).

 **TIMING** 1½ days, including drying time

 **SERVES** 20 finger portions

Equipment

* 23cm (9in) fondant-covered cake drum (p51)
* fondant roller
* multi-ribbon cutter, straight sides
* frilling tool
* 3 decorative stamens
* 1m (3ft) teal satin ribbon (1cm/½in wide)
* craft glue

Ingredients

* 2 x 15cm (6in) vanilla sponge cakes (see p228), halved and sandwiched with buttercream icing
* 500g (1lb 2oz) white fondant and 250g (9oz) white flower paste, kneaded together
* 1 tub blue colouring paste
* cornflour, for dusting
* 200g (7oz) buttercream icing (see pp24–25)
* edible glue

1 A day before serving, transfer the cake onto the covered cake drum. Divide the fondant–flower paste into 5 equal portions. Dip a cocktail stick into the colouring paste and add 1 dot to a portion. Knead it in. Add 2–3 dots of colouring paste to the second portion, and blend, ensuring the colour is deeper than the previous portion. Continue with the final 3 portions, adding increasing amounts of colouring paste, to create darker shades (i.e., 4–5 dots for the third portion, 7–8 dots for the fourth, and ½ tsp for the last). Wrap all of the fondant in cling film.

2 On a cornflour-dusted surface, roll out a small amount of the darkest blue fondant to 2mm (¹⁄₁₆in) thick and cut a strip about 2.5cm (1in) wide with a ribbon cutter. Use a frilling tool to frill one side of the strip. Moisten the unfrilled side and fix to the base of the cake with buttercream icing. Repeat until a row of dark-blue ruffles surrounds the base of the cake.

3 Create a second layer of ruffles, and work upwards around the cake using the rest of the darkest fondant, finishing with a full row. Use the next shade of fondant, and continue ruffling until the entire cake is covered. Use the lightest shade to create 2 layers around the top, and a circle of ruffles on the cake's surface. Leave the cake to rest for a day, and start to model the flower.

4 Knead together the remaining fondant for an even colour. Roll it out on a cornflour-dusted surface to 2mm (¹⁄₁₆in) thick. Cut a 4 x 30cm (1½ x 12in) strip, and gather it to model a flower shape, rolling until the flower is 10cm (4in) wide. Pinch together the fondant at the base and remove excess. Press the stamens into the centre of the flower, and leave to dry overnight. Fix to the top of the cake with a little edible glue. Use craft glue to fix the ribbon around the cake drum.

BRING IT ALL TOGETHER

Using multi-ribbon cutters see p118

Modelling embellishments see p97

CAKE BASICS

Anyone can bake truly delicious cakes. Here are all of the classic recipes – from light sponges, lush Madeira cakes, rich fruitcakes, and moist gingerbread, to miniature cakes, cupcakes, and cake pops. Learn how to bake, test, cool, and level the perfect cake – a flawless canvas for decorating.

Classic vanilla sponge

This sponge makes a good base for many kinds of cakes, and can be adapted to incorporate other flavours. Filled with jam and cream, for instance, it becomes a Victoria sponge cake. Use larger tins for thin layers, and smaller tins for deeper ones.

 **PREP** 20 mins  **COOK** 25-30 mins  **SERVES** 10

Equipment

* 2 x 20cm (8in) round cake tins, greased and lined (see p236)

Ingredients

* 200g (7oz) unsalted butter, softened
* 200g (7oz) caster sugar
* 4 eggs
* 1 tsp vanilla extract
* 200g (7oz) self-raising flour
* 1 tsp baking powder

Variations

A few extra ingredients can transform a basic sponge into something really special. Experiment with other flavours and textures. Add poppy seeds to a lemon cake, or try flavoured fruit and nut extracts like strawberry or almond.

1 Preheat the oven to 180°C (350°F/Gas 4). Whisk the butter and sugar in a bowl for 2 minutes, or until pale and fluffy.

2 Add the eggs, 1 at a time, mixing well. Add the vanilla extract and whisk for 2 minutes, till bubbles appear on the surface.

3 Sift in the flour and baking powder, and gently fold in with a metal spoon, keeping the mixture light and smooth.

To bake

Divide the mixture evenly between the tins and smooth with a palette knife. Bake for 25–30 minutes, or until a skewer comes out clean (see p238).

To finish

Cool the cakes in the tins for a few minutes, then turn out onto a wire rack. When completely cool, fill as desired.

Coffee cake

Coffee cake is a popular celebration cake and a traditional choice for teatime. The only additional ingredient you will need is some strong instant coffee, but you could add walnuts for even more flavour and texture.

Ingredients

* all ingredients for classic vanilla sponge plus:
* 1 tbsp strong instant coffee granules
* 50g (2oz) chopped walnuts, optional
* coffee buttercream icing (see p25)

1 Mix together the strong instant coffee granules with 1 tablespoon of boiling water until dissolved. Allow to cool.

2 Follow steps 1–3 of the classic vanilla sponge recipe opposite, then stir in the cooled coffee mixture. If desired, add the walnuts at the same time, and mix.

3 Continue to follow the recipe. When the cake has cooled, fill and ice with coffee buttercream icing (see p25).

Walnuts *are flavoursome and can also be used for decorating.*

Lemon cake

A surprisingly light variation of the classic vanilla sponge, this is an ideal cake for the summer months. The lemon zest and juice add a tangy touch which cuts through the sweetness well.

Ingredients

* all ingredients for classic vanilla sponge, minus the vanilla extract, plus:
* finely grated zest and juice of 1 lemon
* lemon curd, optional
* lemon buttercream icing (see p25), optional

1 Follow steps 1–3 of the classic vanilla sponge recipe, but stir in the lemon zest and juice in place of the vanilla extract. If you like a particularly strong flavour, zest 2 lemons instead of 1, but use the same amount of lemon juice.

2 Continue to follow the recipe. When the cake has cooled, fill with lemon curd and ice with lemon buttercream icing (see p25), if desired.

Lemon *provides a welcome fresh contrast to icings and coverings.*

Carrot cake

This rich, moist cake is not only easy to make, but works well in stacked and layered projects, as its density helps to support additional weight. Cream cheese buttercream icing (see p25) is the perfect topping. Begin by roasting the walnuts and rubbing them to remove the skins.

 **PREP** 20 mins  **COOK** 45 mins  **SERVES** 10

Equipment

* 23cm (9in) round springform cake tin, greased and lined (see p236)

Ingredients

* 100g (3½oz) walnuts
* 225ml (7½fl oz) sunflower oil
* 3 large eggs
* 225g (8oz) soft light brown sugar
* 1 tsp vanilla extract
* 200g (7oz) carrots, grated
* 100g (3½oz) sultanas
* 200g (7oz) self-raising flour, sifted
* 50g (1¾oz) wholemeal self-raising flour, sifted
* pinch of salt
* 1 tsp ground cinnamon
* 1 tsp ground ginger
* ¼ tsp grated nutmeg
* grated zest of 1 orange

1 Preheat the oven to 180°C (350°F/Gas 4). Roast the walnuts for 5 minutes, rub with a tea towel, and roughly chop.

2 Pour the oil and eggs into a bowl and add the sugar and vanilla extract. Whisk until smooth and thick.

3 Squeeze dry the carrots, and fold into the batter, followed by the walnuts and sultanas. Stir in the remaining ingredients.

To bake

Spread into the tin, using a palette knife to smooth. Bake for 45 minutes, or until a skewer comes out clean (see p238).

To finish

Cool for 10 minutes in the tin, and then transfer to a wire rack to cool completely. If desired, split and fill, or ice the top, with cream cheese buttercream icing (see p25).

Madeira cake

Just a few simple ingredients are needed to create this dense, buttery, lemon-flavoured cake that is ideal for carving and shaping. If you prefer, replace the lemon zest with 1½ teaspoons of vanilla extract or any other flavour of your choice.

 **PREP** 20 mins    **COOK** 50-60 mins    **SERVES** 10

Equipment

* 18cm (7in) round springform cake or 900g (2lb) loaf tin, greased and lined (see p236)

Ingredients

* 175g (6oz) unsalted butter, softened
* 175g (6oz) caster sugar
* 3 eggs
* 225g (8oz) self-raising flour
* grated zest of 1 lemon

Tip
Make sure you use the very best extracts you can find to flavour your cakes. Pure extracts will always have a deeper, more natural taste than synthetic flavourings, and that can make all the difference to the finished cake.

1 Preheat the oven to 180°C (350°F/Gas 4). Whisk the butter and sugar until fluffy. Mix in the eggs, one at a time.

2 Whisk for 2 minutes more, until bubbles appear on the surface. Sift in the flour, add the zest, and fold in until just smooth.

3 Spoon into the tin and bake for about 50–60 minutes, or until a skewer comes out clean (see p238). Leave to cool in the tin for 10 minutes and then turn out onto a wire rack to cool completely.

Chocolate cake

Chocolate cake is an all-time favourite and the yogurt in this recipe makes it extra moist. If you like rich cakes, add another 25g (scant 1oz) of cocoa powder and use crème fraîche in place of yogurt. This cake is delicious with a chocolate or vanilla buttercream (see pp24–25).

 **PREP** 30 mins    **COOK** 20-25 mins    **SERVES** 10

Equipment

* 2 x 18cm (7in) round cake tins, greased and lined (see p236)

Ingredients

* 175g (6oz) unsalted butter, softened
* 175g (6z) soft light brown sugar
* 3 large eggs
* 125g (4½oz) self-raising flour
* 50g (1¾oz) cocoa powder
* 1 tsp baking powder
* 2 tbsp Greek yogurt
* chocolate buttercream icing (see p25)

1 Preheat the oven to 180°C (350°F/Gas 4). Whisk the butter and sugar in a bowl until light and fluffy.

2 Add the eggs one at a time, beating after each addition. In a separate bowl, sift together all of the dry ingredients.

3 Fold the flour mixture into the batter, until well blended. When the batter is light and fluffy, gently fold through the yogurt.

To bake

Divide the mixture between the tins, smoothing the surface with a palette knife. Bake for 20–25 minutes, or until a skewer comes out clean (see p238).

To finish

Cool the cakes in the tins for 5 minutes and then turn onto a wire rack. When cool, fill with chocolate buttercream icing (see p25).

Traditional fruitcake

This rich cake is a popular choice for weddings and festivities. It provides a base for stacked and layered cakes, and covers well with marzipan. Allow enough time to soak the fruit overnight at room temperature, and ensure the cake is baked all the way through (see p238).

 **PREP** 20 mins    **COOK** 3½ hrs    **SERVES** 32

Equipment

* 20cm (8in) deep, round cake tin, with a removable base, greased and lined (see p236)

Ingredients

* 250g (9oz) raisins
* 250g (9oz) sultanas
* 250g (9oz) prunes, chopped
* 115g (4oz) glace cherries, quartered
* 1 dessert apple, peeled, cored, and diced
* 1 tsp ground mixed spice
* zest and juice of 1 orange
* 150ml (5fl oz) sherry or brandy
* 250g (9oz) butter, softened
* 250g (9oz) dark brown sugar
* 4 eggs, lightly beaten
* 60g (2oz) ground almonds
* 250g (9oz) plain flour, sifted

1 Simmer the first 8 ingredients for 5 mins. Remove from the heat and leave to soak for 4 hours or overnight.

3 Gently fold in the fruit mix and almonds. Add the flour and fold in until the ingredients are well mixed.

2 Preheat the oven to 150°C (300°F/Gas 2). Whisk the butter and sugar until fluffy. Mix in the eggs, a little at a time.

To bake

Spoon the mixture into the tin, and cover loosely with baking paper. Then bake for 3½ hours, until the cake is firm to the touch.

To finish

Leave the cake to cool in the tin for 10 minutes, then turn out onto a wire rack to cool completely. If desired, pour a tablespoon of brandy or rum over the cake.

Red velvet cake

This vivid red cake is traditionally topped with cream cheese buttercream icing. Roasted beetroot is used here in place of colouring paste to give the cake its signature colour, but you could stir one teaspoon of red colouring paste in with the beetroot, if desired.

 **PREP** 30 mins    **COOK** 1½ hrs    **SERVES** 10

Equipment

* 2 x 20cm (8in) round cake tins, greased and lined (see p236)

Ingredients

* 3–4 medium beetroots, 500g (1lb 2oz) in total
* 300g (10oz) plain flour
* 50g (1¾oz) cocoa powder
* 2 tsp bicarbonate of soda
* ½ tsp salt
* 175g (6oz) unsalted butter, softened
* 275g (9½oz) brown sugar
* 200g (7oz) caster sugar
* 3 large eggs, at room temperature
* 2 tsp vanilla extract
* 100g (3½oz) dark chocolate, broken into pieces and melted
* 150ml (5fl oz) buttermilk mixed with 2 tsp cider vinegar

1 Cook the beetroot in a pan covered with water for 30–40 minutes. Cool, then peel. Preheat the oven to 180°C (350°F/Gas 4).

2 Whizz to a purée in a food processor, adding a little water if necessary. Sift together the flour, cocoa, bicarbonate, and salt.

3 In a separate bowl, whisk the butter, sugars, eggs, and vanilla, then add the cooled, melted chocolate.

To bake and finish

Slowly add the flour mixture and buttermilk–vinegar mix to the batter. Beat well between additions. Stir in 250ml (9fl oz) of the beetroot purée, and continue to mix. Divide the batter between the tins. Bake for 35 minutes, or until a skewer comes out clean (see p238). Leave to cool, slice each cake in half, and layer with cream cheese buttercream icing (see p25), if desired.

Gingerbread

Firm gingerbread is ideal for creating 3D projects with a template. Before you begin building, allow at least a week for the gingerbread to harden. Gingerbread creations are traditionally "glued" together with royal icing (see pp34–35) or melted, caramelized sugar (see Tip).

 **PREP** 30 mins    **COOK** 15 mins   **MAKES** 800g (1¾lb)

Ingredients

* 175ml (6fl oz) golden syrup
* 115g (4oz) butter
* 115g (4oz) brown sugar
* 600g (1lb 5oz) plain flour, sifted, plus extra for dusting
* 1 tsp ground cinnamon
* 4 tsp ground ginger
* 4 tsp bicarbonate of soda, dissolved in 4 tsp cold water
* 2 egg yolks

Tip

To make sugar "glue", melt 250g (9oz) white granulated sugar in a heavy-based pan over a medium heat, until the sugar melts and browns. Be careful, as it can burn. Spread onto the gingerbread edges to glue pieces together. Beware: it is very hot.

1 Melt the syrup, butter, and sugar in a pan. In a bowl, sift together the flour, cinnamon, and ginger. Make a well in the centre.

3 While the dough is still warm, roll it out to about 5mm (¼in) thick. Preheat the oven to 180°C (350°F/Gas 4).

2 Stir in the soda mix, yolks, and the melted syrup, sugar, and butter. Knead into a pliable dough on a flour-dusted surface.

To shape

Place the template on top of the rolled-out dough, and cut around it using a sharp knife (see p57).

To bake

Carefully lift onto a lightly greased and lined baking tray. Bake for 10–13 minutes, or until firm and just beginning to brown at the edges. Remove from the oven and cool on the tray until required.

Preparing tins

Even the most perfectly baked cakes can be ruined if they stick to the cake tin, so it is essential that you prepare and line the tins properly. This will ensure that your cake can be removed in a smooth manner and cleaning up time will be reduced considerably.

Greasing

Almost all cake tins, including non-stick tins, should be greased with butter, margarine, or oil. Use a pastry brush to ensure even coverage. Silicone pastry brushes are much more hygienic and easier to look after than nylon or bristle brushes. Moulded tins, especially novelty tins (see opposite), need greasing particularly well in the corners and crevices.

Dusting

Tins without a non-stick coating must be dusted with flour, after greasing. Sprinkle 1 tablespoon of plain flour into the bottom of the tin. Hold the tin over the sink, tilt it to move the flour from side to side, and tap the bottom to ensure even coverage. Discard excess flour by inverting the tin and tapping the bottom.

Lining

Using baking parchment helps to prevent burning, particularly for cakes with longer cook times.

1 Grease the tins to ensure that the parchment sticks to the tin and does not move when the batter is poured.

2 Cut a strip of parchment that is slightly longer than the circumference and slightly wider than the height of the tin.

3 Fold the strip about 2.5cm (1in) from the long edge and make some evenly spaced cuts to the fold line.

4 Press the parchment strip into the tin. Cut a circle, using the bottom of the tin as a template, and fit in the base of the tin.

Using a moulded cake tin

Moulded, novelty cake tins come in a variety of shapes, from simple 3D balls to miniature wedding cakes, beehives, giant cupcakes, cars, and sandcastles. If you are not confident enough to carve (see p65), this is an ideal way to achieve the shape you want with minimum fuss.

Ball tins

For basic sponges, grease and dust the tins. Lay them flat on a baking tray and fill nearly to the top with batter. Make sure both halves are level, using scrunched up foil to support. Bake according to instructions on the tin. Allow both halves to cool for 10 minutes in the tin, before trimming uneven edges, and turning out onto a wire rack. When completely cool, sandwich together with buttercream icing (see p28).

For denser batters, prepare the tins, as above, but fill only one tin half, creating a ball shape with your fingers that comes out over the top of the tin. Lock over the other half, and bake it on a baking tray, as above. Cool in the tin, then turn the whole cake out onto a wire rack to cool completely.

Novelty tins

1 After greasing and dusting, pour the batter into the tin so that it is just over three-quarters full. Tap it on a firm surface to release air bubbles and ensure a smooth finish.

2 Bake according to the instructions on the tin. It helps to place the novelty tin on a baking tray for easy removal from the oven, and to catch any overspill while baking. Allow the cake to cool for at least 10 minutes in the tin, before running a knife between the cake and the edge of the tin.

3 Gently turn the cake upside down on a wire rack, and lift the tin off the cake. If the cake has risen unevenly, or the surface of the cake domes in the centre, level it (see p239) before turning it out.

Baking and cooling

Make sure that cakes are cooked at the right temperature and for the correct length of time before you remove them from the oven. This ensures good consistency and optimum rising. It is also crucial to cool the cakes completely before icing, filling, or decorating.

Baking

Preheat the oven for 20 minutes before baking. Fan or convection ovens require a lower temperature. If the recipe does not specify this, reduce the temperature by about 20°C (25°F). Give the tin a few knocks against a hard surface before it goes into the oven, to release air bubbles. Don't open the oven – changes in temperature cause cakes to sink. If your oven heats unevenly, turn the cake after three-quarters of the cooking time. Cook for the entire time suggested by the recipe.

Testing

There are two main ways to test a cake. The first is to press gently down in the centre of the cake with your finger. If it springs back, chances are it is ready. To be certain, insert a metal or wooden skewer into the centre of the cake (pop it into a crack to avoid blemishing the surface). If it comes out clean, the cake is ready. Novelty cakes can take longer to bake, so be sure to check the recommended time on the recipe on the tin packaging.

Cooling

Cool a cake in its tin for about 10 minutes (a little longer if it is a deep, large cake), helping the cake to keep its shape and "set". Then turn it out onto one wire rack, and then invert it onto another rack to cool completely. The base of your cake should be on the rack, not the top, to prevent it from losing its height and texture. Always make sure the cake is cool before icing and plating it, as this will prevent crumbling, breakage, and movement. If you are in a rush, you can chill your cake after it has been cooled in the tin.

Levelling

For a perfect finish, it is important to level the cake. If there are only a few uneven bits, wait until it has cooled in the tin for 10 minutes, and then gently trim them off with a knife. If the cake is lopsided or lumpy, allow it to cool completely on a wire rack before levelling it.

Turntable method

Place the cake on a cake board, and then on top of a turntable or lazy Susan. If it is not the board you will be using for the finished cake, dust it first with icing sugar to ensure that the cake will not stick. Use a ruler and cocktail sticks pressed into the cake to mark your cutting line, to be sure it is even all the way round. Carefully turn the stand and gently move a serrated knife back and forth in a sawing motion to remove the dome. Some people find it easier to partially freeze the cakes before levelling, which prevents chunks of cake being drawn up when you "saw" through it.

Cake leveller method

If you have a cake leveller, place the cake on a cake board, over a firm surface, and carefully position the blade at the appropriate height. Gently saw into the side using a back and forth motion. Once you have got past the crust, simply glide the blade through the cake to the other side. If you are finding it tricky to keep the cake still while you cut, you can place it on a board exactly the same size as the cake, and pop the cake, on the board, back into the cake tin. Level across the cake using the top edge of the tin.

Making cupcakes

Be sure to fill the tins or cases properly and cook for the correct length of time. Always preheat the oven for at least 20 minutes. Prepare the tins before you begin to make the batter, so that it doesn't begin to rise before you put it into the cases.

Using cases

Cupcake cases add a decorative element, make the cupcakes look neater, and help them remain fresh and moist for longer. If you choose to use a cupcake tin on its own, grease and dust it, brush with cake release products, or spray with a non-stick baking spray. Silicone cases do not require a cupcake tin. Fill and set them upright on a baking tray. Grease and dust them with plain flour to ensure that the cupcakes do not stick.

Filling

Fill the cupcake cases or tins about two-thirds full. Do not overfill as they can spill over the sides or develop a "nose". Standard-sized cupcakes require about 75ml (2½fl oz) of batter. For mini cupcakes, a heaped tablespoon of batter is enough. For special effects, layer different colours of batter into the cases with a piping bag. Create a surprise centre by popping sweets or even a biscuit or a miniature brownie into the centre before cooking.

Baking

A standard-sized cupcake will take 18–20 minutes to bake, while mini cupcakes will take 8–10 minutes. They are ready if a skewer inserted in the middle of the cake comes out clean. When baking several tins at the same time, increase the baking time by a few minutes, and rotate the trays halfway through. Allow to cool in the tin for at least 10 minutes and then cool on a wire rack. If you do not use cases, turn the cupcakes out onto your hand before placing them on the rack.

Baking miniature cakes

Make miniature ("mini") cakes in the same way as cupcakes, but bake them in specially designed round or square cake tins. Grease and dust the tins carefully. You could use deep cutters or a knife to cut mini cakes from a large cake, but this is not as accurate and you may waste cake.

 **PREP** 20 mins    **COOK** 15 mins    **MAKES** 16

Equipment

* 16 x 5cm (2in) mini round cake tins

Ingredients

* 1 x quantity of Madeira cake batter (see p231)

1 Preheat the oven to 190°C (375°F/Gas 5). Fill all of the tins with the same amount of batter – roughly half to two-thirds full.

2 Mini cakes take 15–25 minutes to bake, depending on their size, so check the instructions on the cake tin.

3 When they look like they may be done, test every two minutes until a skewer comes out clean (see p238). Allow the cakes to cool in the tins and then turn out onto a wire rack.

Tips
Bake cupcakes as soon as the batter is ready. This will ensure that the air in the mixture does not escape, resulting in flatter cupcakes. Cupcakes and mini cakes can be decorated, once cool, with a variety of toppings (see pp32–33).

Divide the mix *equally between the tins. Trim the cakes when they have cooled, if necessary.*

Making cake pops

Cake pops are relative newcomers to the baking arena and offer a perfect opportunity to accessorize cakes and create a decorative theme (see p223). There are two ways to make cake pops. This method uses up leftover cake – easily moulded into balls, hearts, or even critters.

 **PREP** 4 hrs    **MAKES** 20-25

Equipment

* 25 cake-pop sticks
* florist oasis or Styrofoam

Ingredients

* 300g (10oz) chocolate cake crumbs
* 150g (5½oz) chocolate buttercream icing (see pp24–25)
* 250g (9oz) dark chocolate cake covering
* 50g (1¾oz) white chocolate
* 300g (10oz) candy melts (optional, to replace dark and white chocolate)
* sprinkles, nuts, or ground wafers, to decorate, optional

1 Place the cake crumbs in a large bowl, and stir in the buttercream icing, mixing until you have a smooth dough.

2 Using your hands, gently mould the mixture into uniform balls, each the approximate size of a walnut.

3 Place on a plate, with space between each, and refrigerate for 3 hours; alternatively, you can freeze for 30 minutes.

To cover

Line two trays with baking parchment and melt some dark chocolate covering. Dip one end of a cake-pop stick into the chocolate and insert into the centre of each pop. Stand them upright in florist oasis for 30 minutes. Melt the rest of the chocolate covering and white chocolate, or candy melts. Dip the pops into the chocolate and swirl to cover. Allow excess to drip off, and dip them in sprinkles, nuts, or ground wafers, if desired.

Using a cake-pop tin

Cake-pop tins look like miniature "ball tins" (see p237). Use them to create uniform balls that are ready to dip and decorate. Light sponges are not dense enough to support the weight of the pop on a stick, or the decorations. Madeira cake is a better option. Most cake-pop tins come with recipes.

 **PREP** 20 mins    **COOK** 15-18 mins    **MAKES** 12

Equipment

* 12-hole cake-pop tin

Ingredients

* plain flour, for dusting
* ½ quantity Madeira cake batter (see p231)
* melted chocolate

1 Preheat the oven to 180°C (350°F/Gas 4). Grease and dust the tins. Spoon the batter into the bottom half of the tin (without holes) so that it mounds over the top of the tin. Every cake pop tin is different, so follow the specific instructions to ensure you use the correct amount of batter.

2 Place the top half of the tin on top and secure with keys. Bake for 15–18 minutes. After baking time, test every two minutes until a skewer comes out clean. Allow the cakes to cool in the tin for ten minutes and then turn out onto a wire rack to cool completely.

3 Chill the cake pops before decorating, so that they to keep their shape. First, dip one end of a cake-pop stick into a little melted chocolate and insert into the centre of each pop. Chill for 20–30 minutes, with the sticks upright. Cover, as described opposite.

Tip
To keep the chocolate or candy melts warm and in a liquid state while dipping, use a fondue pot or place the pan on a tea-light burner. Using a taller, narrow pan makes dipping easier and much less messy.

Cool cake pops *in the tin before inserting the cake-pop sticks.*

Templates

Templates ensure that you have an accurate pattern for 3D constructions and decorations. You can enlarge or reduce the scale of them to suit the size of any cake. Each of the templates here has an enlargement percentage that will help you to scale them to individual projects.

Runout robin
Use these templates for separate runouts. They sit on top of the Festive fruitcake (see pp220–21).

Complete robin body, scan 1 at 200%.

Robin's little wing, scan 1 at 200%.

Tip
Use a photocopier or a scanner to enlarge templates appropriately, and then print and cut them out, or you could trace and enlarge by hand. If desired, trace them out onto baking parchment, which doesn't stick to modelling pastes.

Newborn topper
This template forms the fondant topper to the Newborn celebration cake (see pp192–93).

Heart-shaped topper, scan 1 at 200%.

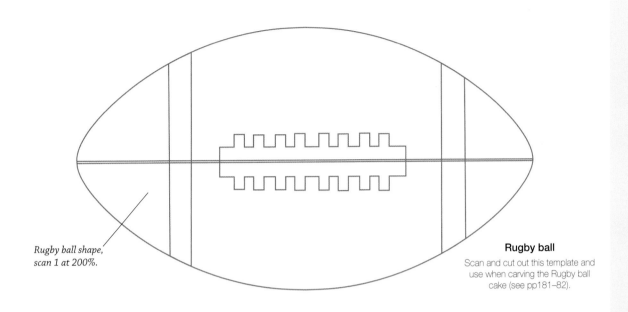

Rugby ball shape, scan 1 at 200%.

Rugby ball

Scan and cut out this template and use when carving the Rugby ball cake (see pp181–82).

Scalloped-edge marker, scan multiples at 200%.

Scalloped-edge marker

Scan, cut out, and tape together multiples of this template, so that every tier on the Filigree wedding cake (see pp214–16) has a template to mark the top of the filigree piping.

Princess garden template, scan 1 at 400%.

Princess garden marker

Scan, cut out, and use to measure out the rolling fields around the Princess castle cake (see pp170–75).

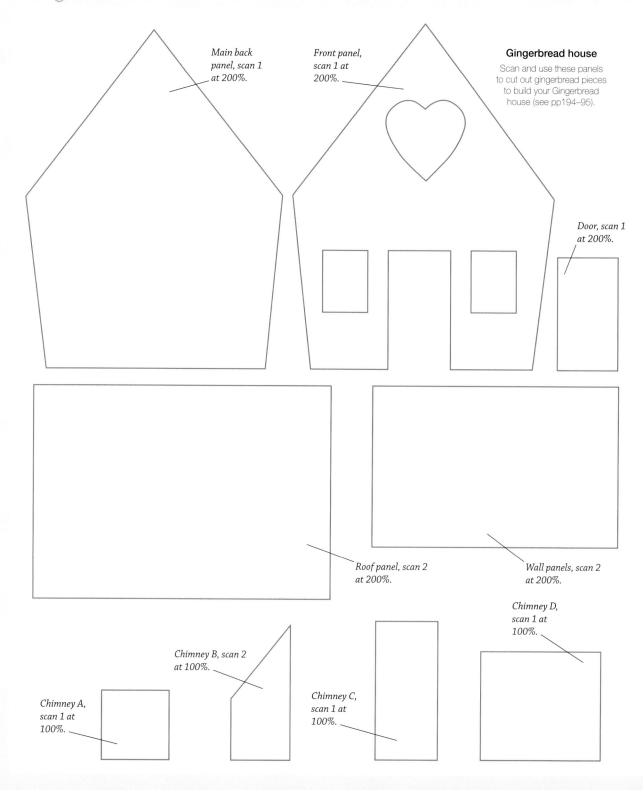

Main back panel, scan 1 at 200%.

Front panel, scan 1 at 200%.

Gingerbread house

Scan and use these panels to cut out gingerbread pieces to build your Gingerbread house (see pp194–95).

Door, scan 1 at 200%.

Roof panel, scan 2 at 200%.

Wall panels, scan 2 at 200%.

Chimney D, scan 1 at 100%.

Chimney B, scan 2 at 100%.

Chimney C, scan 1 at 100%.

Chimney A, scan 1 at 100%.

About the contributors

Karen Sullivan is a writer, editor, and bespoke cake-maker with a successful celebration cake business in London, UK. She learned to bake as a toddler, in her grandmother's kitchen in Canada, and has honed her decorating skills over the years. She creates unique and highly sought-after cakes for a range of occasions.

Asma Hassan is the owner of The Sugared Saffron Cake Company, specializing in modern wedding cakes and dessert tables. She is a self-taught cake decorator whose work features in bridal and sugarcraft publications.
Her work features on p1; pp4–5; p6; p7 (Teddy bear mini cakes); p23 (Butterfly cupcakes); p45; p54; p72; pp76–77; p100; p124; p163; pp184–85 (Butterfly cupcakes); pp190–91; pp196–97; pp198–201; pp205–07; pp210–13; and pp224–25.

www.sugaredsaffron.co.uk

Sandra Monger is an award-winning cake designer based in Bath, UK, who specializes in bespoke wedding and celebration cakes. Professionally trained in advanced pâtisserie and sugarcraft, she also teaches cake-decorating courses.
Her work features on p2; p7 (Princess cake pops); p23 (Blossom cupcakes); pp26–27; p32; pp38–39; p43; p55; p56; p85; p86; pp92–93; p97 (ruffles); p141; p147; p148; p152; p156; p162; pp170–75; pp180–83; pp184–85 (Blossom cupcakes); pp192–93; pp194–95; pp208–09; pp214–17; pp220–23; p226; p227; and p247.

www.sandramongercakes.co.uk

Amelia Nutting is an award-winning cake decorator and owner of Shuga Budz, a family-run cake decorating company based in Wolverhampton, UK. For the last six years she has been entering national decorating competitions and teaching courses to decorating enthusiasts of all ages.
Her work features on p3; p22; pp82–83; pp90–91; pp94–95; pp104–05; p109; pp132–33; p134; p143; pp164–66; pp167–69; pp176–79; pp202–04; and pp218–19.

www.facebook.com/shuga.budz

Adapting cake quantities

To adapt recipes for cakes of any size and shape, multiply the batches of batter you make. Test cakes regularly to ensure they are perfectly baked – large cakes require the most time.

Cake tin	Multiple of basic recipe		Cooking time		Marzipan or ready-to-roll icing to cover	Liquid capacity of tin
	Sponge cake	Fruitcake	Sponge cake at 180°C (350°F/Gas 4)	Fruitcake at 160°C (325°F/Gas 3)		
ROUND CAKE TINS						
15 x 6cm (6 x 2½in)	1	½	25–30 mins	2½ hrs	350g/12oz	1.1 litres/2 pints
18 x 7cm (7 x 2¾in)	1½	¾	30–35 mins	2½–3 hrs	550g/1¼lb	1.8 litres/3¼ pints
20 x 7.5cm (8 x 3in)	2	1	35–40 mins	3½–4 hrs	600g/1lb 5oz	2.4 litres/4¼ pints
23 x 8cm (9 x 3¼in)	2½	1¼	40–45 mins	4½–5 hrs	800g/1¾lb	3.3 litres/5¾ pints
25.5 x 9cm (10 x 3½in)	3½	1½	50–55 mins	5½ hrs	900g/2lb	4.6 litres/8 pints
28 x 9.5cm (11 x 3¾in)	–	2¼	–	6 hrs	1.1kg/2½lb	5.9 litres/10½ pints
30 x 10cm (12 x 4in)	–	3½	–	6½–7 hrs	1.5kg/3lb 3oz	7.1 litres/12½ pints
35.5 x 11.5cm (14 x 4½in)	–	4¼	–	7½–8 hrs	1.8kg/4lb	11.4 litres/20 pints
SQUARE CAKE TINS						
15 x 6cm (6 x 2½in)	1½	¾	30–35 mins	2½ hrs	500g/1lb	1.4 litres/2½ pints
18 x 7cm (7 x 2¾in)	2	1	35–40 mins	2½–3 hrs	700g/1½lb	2.3 litres/4 pints
20 x 7.5cm (8 x 3in)	2½	1¼	40–45 mins	3½–4 hrs	800g/1¾lb	3 litres/5¼ pints
23 x 8cm (9 x 3¼in)	3¼	1½	50–55 mins	4½–5 hrs	900g/2lb	4.2 litres/7½ pints
25.5 x 9cm (10 x 3½in)	4	2¼	60–65 mins	5½ hrs	1.1kg/2½lb	5.9 litres/10½ pints
28 x 9.5cm (11 x 3¾in)	–	3	–	6 hrs	1.5kg/3lb 3oz	7.4 litres/13 pints
30 x 10cm (12 x 4in)	–	4¼	–	6½–7 hrs	1.8kg/4lb	9 litres/15¾ pints
35.5 x 11.5cm (14 x 4½in)	–	5	–	7½–8 hrs	2kg/4½lb	14.5 litres/25½ pints

Unusual tins

If baking in an unusually shaped tin, such as a hexagon, heart, or oval, measure the capacity of the tin by filling it with water (if it has a loose base you will have to line the tin with a plastic bag) and emptying into a measuring jug. Then use the chart to find the tin with the same or nearest liquid capacity, and use the quantities given for that cake size.

Baking large cakes

When baking cakes over 25.5cm (10in) in width, reduce the oven temperature by 10°C (15°F/1 Gas mark) two-thirds of the way through the cooking time. For cakes of this size it is also advisable to line the tin with brown paper or baking parchment before pouring in the batter, to avoid letting the edges of the cake burn while the centre is still cooking.

Resources

UK RESOURCES

Windsor Cake Craft
A comprehensive and exciting range
of decorating supplies.
211 Europa Boulevard
Gemini Business Park
Warrington
WA5 7TN
01925 444590
www.windsorcakecraft.co.uk

Cake Craft World
With two shops, in southeast London and
Kent, and a fantastic range of supplies online,
Cake Craft World is well worth a visit.
Unit 8, North Downs Business Park
Pilgrims Way (Lime Pit Lane)
Sevenoaks
Kent TN13 2TL
01732 463573
www.cakecraftworld.co.uk

Sugarshack
A veritable treasure-trove of cake-decorating
ingredients, and everything cake-related.
Unit 12 Bowmans Trading Estate
Westoreland Road
London NW9 9RL
0208 204 2994
www.sugarshack.co.uk

Surbiton Sugarcraft
A range of cake-decorating supplies and
equipment, including handmade sugar flowers.
140 Hook Road
Surbiton
Surrey KT6 5BZ
0208 391 4664
www.surbitonart.co.uk

Cakes, Cookies, and Craft Shop
A one-stop shop, online or in person, for
everything from equipment to chocolate.
Unit 2 Francis Business Park
White Lund Industrial Estate,
Morecambe
Lancashire LA3 3PT
01524 389684
www.cakescookiesandcraftsshop.co.uk

Cake Stuff
Virtually everything cake-related at one site.
Milton Industrial Estate,
Lesmahagow
ML11 0JN Scotland
01555 890111
www.cake-stuff.com

The Cake Decorating Company
Find everything you need in one place for
making, baking, and decorating fantastic cakes.
Unit 2b Triumph Road
Nottingham NG7 2GA
0115 969 9800
www.thecakedecoratingcompany.co.uk

Squires Kitchen
Excellent shop and site for inspiration and
a huge range of cake decorating supplies.
3 Waverley Lane
Farnham
Surrey GU9 8BB
0845 61 71 810 or 01252 260 260
www.squires-shop.com

Knightsbridge PME School
of Cake Decorating
Excellent programme of classes teaching wide
variety of cake decoration skills and techniques.
23 Riverwalk Road
Brimsdown
Enfield
EN3 7QN
0203 234 0049
www.knightsbridgepmeschoolofcakedecorating.co.uk

Cake Decorating Store
An online shop and resource with a selection
of decorating tools, ingredients, and decorations.
Unit C4 Burley Hill Trading Estate
Burley Road
Leeds
LS4 2PU
0845 6525 357
www.cakedecoratingstore.co.uk

The Little Cake Shop
Online store with a fantastic range of everything
cake-related, with a handy blog for ideas.
Unit B140
Riverside
Bendon Valley
London SW18 4UQ
0208 871 0105
www.thelittlecakeshop.co.uk

Sugarcraft Boutique
A small shop with helpful staff and an online store.
If you don't see what you want, order it and they
deliver within days.
491 Lordship Lane
Dulwich
London SE22 8JY
0208 693 1718
www.sugarcraftboutique.co.uk

AUSTRALIAN RESOURCES

Australian Cake Decorating Network
A networking website with its own magazine,
product reviews, tutorials, and business advice.
www.austcakedecoratingnetwork.com

Cake Deco
Cake Deco is the best known cake-decorating
supply store in Melbourne.
Shop 7, Port Philip Arcade
232 Flinders Street
Melbourne, Victoria
(03) 9654 5335
www.cakedeco.com.au

Glasshouse Cakes and Supplies
Online and retail store, with a vast range
of products including unfinished cakes.
13b Selems Parade
Revesby
NSW 2212
(02) 9773 5513
www.glasshousecakes.com.au

Cakes Around Town
A comprehensive range of decorating supplies
from all over the world.
Unit 2/12 Sudbury Street
Darra
Brisbane, Queensland 4076
(07) 3160 8728
www.cakesaroundtown.com.au

The Spotted Apron
A broad and constantly updated range of supplies
available, including seven-tier cupcake stands.
Merriwa
Perth
Western Australia
(04) 0890 8949
www.thespottedapron.com.au

Complete Cake Decorating Supplies
A comprehensive range of supplies available
for wholesale and retail customers.
63 Boothby Street
Panorama
South Australia 5041
(08) 8299 0333
www.completecake.com.au

Index

Page numbers in **bold** indicate step-by-step techniques and those in *italic* indicate complete cake projects.

Acknowledgments

The author would like to thank three of the most inspiring, delightful, and imaginative cake decorators around: Asma Hassan, Sandra Monger, and Amelia Nutting. Their help in producing gorgeous projects and advising on the techniques has been invaluable. I've learned more from them in four months than I have in five years of cake decorating. Thank you to the DK team, who have worked wonders to produce a lovely, dynamic, and truly helpful book; in particular, Martha Burley is probably the most organised, efficient, and accommodating editor on the face of the earth; Kathryn Wilding has created a superb design and was forever willing to tinker in order to get in all the things we needed. Peggy Vance saw promise in the idea; Charis Bhagianathan, Janashree Singha, Dawn Henderson, and Christine Keilty helped it to come to fruition. Thank you all. Special thanks must go to Rosa Viacava, whose "RVO" lace moulds were shipped from Peru to feature in this book.

DK would like to thank Karen Sullivan, Asma Hassan, Sandra Monger, and Amelia Nutting for their creative cake decorating and inspiration. They would also like to thank the following:

Photography Clive Bozzard-Hill
Additional photography William Reavell
Art direction Penny Stock
Home economist Paul Jackman
Prop styling Liz Hippisley
Proofreading Corinne Masciocchi and Sue Morony
Indexing Vanessa Bird
Design assistance Tessa Bindloss, Kate Fenton, Lucy Parissi, and Harriet Yeomans
Editorial assistance Elizabeth Clinton